CRISIS
of Abundance
RETHINKING HOW WE PAY FOR HEALTH CARE

CRISIS
of Abundance
RETHINKING HOW WE PAY FOR HEALTH CARE

ARNOLD KLING

CATO INSTITUTE
WASHINGTON, D.C.

Library of Congress Cataloging-in-Publication Data

Kling, Arnold S.
  Crisis of abundance : rethinking how we pay for health care / Arnold Kling.
    p. cm.
  Includes bibliographical references.
  ISBN 1-930865-89-9 (alk. paper) 978-1-933995-13-7 (paperback)
  1. Medical care, cost of—United States. 2. Health care reform—United
States. 3. Medical economics—United States. I. Title.

RA410.53.K586 2006
338.4′33621—dc22   2006043904

Cover design by Jon Meyers.
Printed in the United States of America.

CATO INSTITUTE
1000 Massachusetts Ave., N.W.
Washington, D.C. 20001
www.cato.org

Contents

Acknowledgments

Brink Lindsey approached me with the idea of writing a book on health care financing policy, and he then gave me a free hand in creating it. Michael Cannon was extremely generous with his time, sending me topical articles, thoroughly reading the manuscript several times, and making a number of suggestions that greatly improved the final product. Others who provided helpful comments included Iain Murray, Robin Hanson, Tyler Cowen, Alex Tabarrok, Bob Graboyes, and Peter Van Doren. Adrienne Aldredge and others at Cato also provided important support.

I would like to express my appreciation to the technical team at the Agency for Health Research and Quality for making the Medical Expenditure Panel Survey information accessible via the World Wide Web in such a user-friendly manner. This is an instance in which a Cato author feels compelled to acknowledge the existence of a public good.

Notwithstanding all of the valuable assistance I received, any errors of fact or analysis are solely my own.

Preface to Paperback Edition

For the paperback edition of *Crisis of Abundance*, I thought I would step back and describe how my thinking evolved before, during, and after writing the book.

I started thinking about health care by focusing on a well-known puzzle. Over the past 30 years, the United States has increased its health care spending dramatically relative to other countries but without gaining on other countries in terms of longevity. We have tried a "surge" in medical spending, and the surge does not appear to be working.

I started out by looking for evidence that the surge is working. Longevity statistics today are heavily influenced by people born in the 1930s. Perhaps those of us born after 1950 have received more benefits from the surge, and these benefits will show up later. But I did not find any convincing signs of this.

Instead, I came across considerable evidence that suggests that more health care does not necessarily lead to better health. Many studies of comparable populations within the United States receiving different levels of medical services show no difference in outcomes. I interpret this evidence as showing that Americans make extravagant use of medical procedures with high costs and low benefits.

The main empirical finding of the book is that the surge reflects an increase in the use of specialists and high-tech medical equipment. A disturbing fact is that many procedures, such as getting an MRI and an orthopaedic consult for a back injury, are neither absolutely necessary nor absolutely unnecessary. Such procedures instead fall into a gray area, where cost-effectiveness is difficult to determine yet important to take into account.

The second half of the book offers suggestions for health care reforms that would give consumers the means and the motive to weigh costs and benefits more carefully. I recommend a "medical guidelines commission" to rigorously study common medical procedures from a statistical and economic standpoint. I recommend health insurance policies with higher deductibles to give consumers more of an incentive to focus on cost-effectiveness.

So far, the first half of the book has been better received than the second half. Many health policy experts across the ideological spectrum accept the diagnosis. But, apart from the "medical guidelines commission," my suggestions for a cure have drawn less support.

This reception, which was not a surprise, has led me to think harder about the values and beliefs that Americans have about health care. Our values and beliefs make health care reform difficult. After all, neither those who favor a single-payer health care system nor those who prefer much less government in health care are making much headway. The status quo, even though not sustainable, remains attractive.

As I point out in the chapter "no perfect health care system," we want our health care system to have three characteristics: unfettered access to medical services (no rationing or supply constraints); personal insulation from health care costs (paying for medical services through insurance rather than out of pocket); and economic efficiency (cost-effective, sustainable health care finance). At most, we can have two of these three features.

Why is there push-back against proposals to move toward economic efficiency? First, I think that there is a lot of natural resistance to thinking about health care in terms of costs and benefits. We find it somewhat repulsive to bring the topic of money into a discussion of a personal service related to our bodies. We like to speak of the *gift* of healing, not the business of healing.

Moreover, we are reluctant to think in terms of uncertainty, ambiguity, and probability. Instead, we wish to think of health care in black and white, as either necessary or unnecessary. If you don't need it, then you don't get it. And if you need it, there is no interest in doing a cost-benefit calculation.

The truth is that there is a large gray area (think again of the MRI after a back injury), where procedures are neither absolutely necessary nor absolutely unnecessary. There is no escaping that somebody has to make a difficult decision in these gray-area cases.

As it stands today, Americans' values and beliefs tilt the decision in the direction of undertaking more health care procedures. We want to see our ailments tackled immediately, rather than waiting.

We want the doctor to be sure to get the diagnosis right, rather than simply going on superficial evidence.

We never give up. If I cannot do as much with my shoulder as I could when I was 25, then there has to be a way to fix it. If someone has a seemingly fatal illness, then there must be a doctor with a cure.

Our medical system has come to reflect these values and beliefs. In many ways, such values are admirable. However, real health care reform, aimed at obtaining a reasonable balance between costs and benefits, may require confronting and changing some of these values. Keep that in mind as you read the second half of the book.

Arnold Kling

Preface to First Edition

Health care costs affect us as consumers, as workers, as shareholders, and as taxpaying citizens. Why are health care costs rising so rapidly? What are the tradeoffs involved in choosing different ways to pay for health care? How can we improve efficiency and equity in the health care system?

The goal of this book is to present a reasonable set of answers to those questions, and to provide factual and analytical background for policy discussions concerning how we pay for health care and how that affects the availability and quality of health care. The goal is not to press a specific set of solutions or proposals, but to articulate an economic perspective on the issues involved. An economic perspective is important because much of the uneasiness about health care in the United States today relates to cost. The questions posed are ones that an economist can attempt to investigate.

In preparing this book, I reviewed some of the voluminous academic and policy literature, and I tried to assemble data that could help shed light on important issues. In some cases, I found the statistics that I was looking for in the literature. In a few cases, I was able to work with source data to develop answers. In other cases, it seems that we have to do without definitive data for now.

The audience for this book is the concerned citizen. The analysis is intended to be credible to professional economists while readable for noneconomists. I hope that everyone who reads this book, economist and noneconomist alike, will be able to take away useful insights.

Introduction

> I cared for a woman of 23 who complained of back pain for
> months before a neurologist ordered an MRI, expecting to
> find a herniated disc. Instead he found ovarian cancer spread
> to the spine. . . . The patient, treated with extensive surgery
> and chemotherapy, was one of the "lucky cures."
>
> Dr. Mark Siegel[1]

Health care is not what it used to be. Today, many people with
back pain are sent for magnetic resonance imaging, or an MRI. Thirty
years ago, this was not the case.

In 1975, the health care available to a typical middle-class American family was reasonably good. Antibiotics cured infections. Vacci-
nations prevented diseases that had been scourges for earlier genera-
tions. Childbirth was fairly safe, for both the mother and the infant.

A number of diseases had been essentially conquered, including
polio and tuberculosis. Pneumonia and flu, which caused significant
deaths earlier in this century, were responsible for few fatalities
by 1975.

By 1975, deaths from cardiovascular disease among people aged
45–64, which were more than 600 per 100,000 people in the 1940s
and 1950s, had plunged to slightly more than 400 per 100,000. Note
that this is not due solely to better medical care. Other factors, such
as better working conditions and earlier retirement, probably also
played a role.

The high quality of health care in 1975 was reflected in national
health statistics. Infant mortality, which by the 1940s was already
low, fell another 50 percent by 1975, so that only 1.5 percent of
infants failed to survive their first year. Life expectancy at birth was
estimated to have increased from around 66.5 in 1945 to about 72.5
in 1975. Again, bear in mind that factors other than health care
contributed to lower infant mortality and to greater life expectancy.[2]

1

The American middle class can still afford the wonderful health care that was available in 1975—easily. Imagine that a health insurance company today could offer a policy that only covered medical procedures and treatments that were standard in 1975. In 1975, per capita health care spending in today's dollars was about half of what it is today, which suggests that our hypothetical health insurance policy would cost 50 percent less than health insurance today. If so, then it would be affordable for all but the poorest of the poor.

Although we would have little difficulty paying for the health care of 1975, the health care of 2005 and beyond poses a challenge. We read about record numbers of individuals without health insurance. Large corporations are staggering under the weight of the cost of health benefits for retirees and employees. Medicaid (the joint federal-state health care program for the poor) is crowding out other priorities in state budgets, and Medicare (the federal health care program for the elderly) looms as the biggest threat to fiscal balance at the federal level.

I am not going to advocate a policy of returning American health care to the state of the art in 1975.[3] However, as a thought experiment, a return to 1975 health care standards would completely resolve what is commonly described as America's health care crisis. Using only what health care was available in 1975, our large government programs, Medicare and Medicaid, would not be placing government budgets in peril. Employer-provided health insurance would not be the fastest-rising component of worker compensation. Those who are self-employed would find health insurance more affordable, and those who forgo health insurance would be less likely to face medical bills that represent a crushing financial burden.

The difference between 2005 and 1975 is not the result of a price increase (although prices for health care services have increased faster than other prices over this period). It is primarily a difference in the way that medicine is practiced. Thirty years ago, Dr. Siegel's patient would not have been given an MRI, because that technology was not available. In 2005 Americans received more than 24 million MRI examinations, at a cost of hundreds of dollars each. We had arthroscopic knee surgeries, colonoscopies, laser eye surgeries, as well as countless other procedures and treatments that were rare or nonexistent in 1975. We were much more likely to visit a neurologist, allergist, or other specialist than we were 30 years ago.

The medical industry now employs much higher levels of both physical capital (such as diagnostic equipment) and human capital

Table 1
HEALTH CARE SPENDING AS A SHARE OF GDP, SELECT NATIONS, 1980 AND 2002

Country	Health Care as a Percent of GDP, 1980	Health Care as a Percent of GDP, 2002
Canada	7.1	9.6
France	7.1	9.7
Germany	8.7	10.9
United Kingdom	5.6	7.7
United States	8.7	14.6

SOURCE: Organization for Economic Cooperation and Development, "OECD Health Data 2005—Frequently Requested Data," http://www.oecd.org/document/16/0,2340,en_2649_34631_2085200_1_1_1_1,00.html.

(as represented by skilled specialists). This increased supply of human and physical capital is what made the health care of 2005 such a challenge for our household, corporate, and government budgets. If the United States faces a health care crisis today, it is a crisis of abundance.

Financing Premium Medicine

The term I use for American medical care today, with its heavy use of specialists and advanced technology, is "premium medicine." We know that premium medicine costs more than the medical care of 30 years ago. However, we can be less sure how often premium medicine makes a difference in health outcomes.

No society has "solved" the problem of health care finance in the context of premium medicine. It is true that between 1980 and 2002 the share of health care spending in GDP rose more in the United States than it did in other countries (see Table 1). However, countries that have restrained spending have also slowed the adoption of premium medicine through budgetary limits. It is possible that slowing the adoption of premium medicine in that way is a good approach, but it is likely that there are better strategies for balancing the benefits of premium medicine with its costs.

In any case, we probably ought to take the growth in physical and human capital in medical practice as given. We should look at strategies for financing health care in that context.

Overview

Chapter 1, "The Rise of Premium Medicine," shows that the primary driver of the crisis in health care finance is the evolution of the practice of medicine. Over the past few decades, medical care has become more specialized and capital intensive.

Premium medicine consists of

- Frequent referrals to specialists
- Extensive use of high-tech diagnostic procedures
- Increased number and variety of surgeries

In addition to the narrative that attributes the rise in health care spending to premium medicine, there are two other important competing narratives. Chapter 2, "Three Health Care Narratives," compares the premium medicine narrative with a narrative that suggests that private health insurance breaks down because of adverse selection, and a narrative that suggests that health care costs are high because of price-gouging by suppliers. The alternative narratives are inconsistent with some important facts about our health care system.

A notable characteristic of premium medicine is that it often does not affect the outcome. The specialist does not necessarily alter the treatment plan. The MRI may fail to show anything. The surgery may not prevent the patient from dying within a few months.

In a small proportion of cases, such as Dr. Siegel's patient with ovarian cancer, premium medicine does provide clear benefits. However, it is difficult to know in advance who will benefit. In the population as a whole, where those benefits will fall is more concentrated and unpredictable than where the costs will fall. Usually, MRIs undertaken on patients with lower back pain turn up nothing that affects the treatment plan.

Because premium medicine does not always make a difference, its benefits must be evaluated statistically. Chapter 3, "Dollars and Decisions," looks at the principles involved in calculating the value of a procedure based on the probability of that procedure resulting in a benefit to the patient. Contrary to the common misconception, health care is not a black-and-white issue in which people obtain only those services that are clearly necessary. Instead, many health care services fall in a gray area, where the benefits may or may not exceed the costs. Chapter 3 explains some of the subtleties and complexities of such calculations.

Chapter 4, "No Perfect Health Care System," argues that there is a conflict among three major goals for health care finance:

- Affordability for society as a whole
- Unfettered access for individuals
- Insulation of individuals from the costs of health care

If consumers were to have unfettered access while enjoying insulation from cost, the system would not be affordable. Affordability might be achieved through rationing, but that would mean sacrificing unfettered access.

Chapter 5, "Insulation vs. Insurance," illustrates the difference between health insurance as we have come to know it and what would represent real health insurance. The goal of real health insurance should not be complete insulation of the consumer from health care costs. Real health insurance would protect consumers only against catastrophic losses. Premium medicine makes it more important for consumers to understand and adopt true health insurance versus insulation.

Chapter 6, "Matching Funding Systems to Needs," applies the idea of real health insurance to different health care consumers, using data from the U.S. government's Medical Expenditure Panel Survey. The chapter looks at three population groups:

- The very poor, who find health insurance difficult to afford
- People over age 65, who face increased need for health care
- All the rest, who need something like true health insurance

A scheme is developed to replace employer-provided health insurance and Medicare with catastrophic health insurance and savings.

Given that the United States already has a larger proportion of privately financed health care than other industrial countries, why expand that share further? Chapter 7, "Markets and Evolution," points out that in an environment of ongoing change, markets tend to do relatively well at discarding failed and outmoded practices and institutions.

Chapter 8, "Policy Ideas," offers additional proposals to deal with the issue of premium medicine. One proposal is for a Medical Guidelines Commission that would study the cost-effectiveness of medical protocols. Such a commission could recommend standard guidelines for ordering specialist referrals, diagnostic procedures, surgical procedures, and other components of premium medicine. Another proposal is to foster the development of a single point of accountability for an individual's health care. This in turn would facilitate other improvements that would promote efficiency, such as electronic medical records.

Overall, however, it is not my goal to push particular policy proposals. The purpose of this book is to provide useful facts and sound economic analysis to anyone interested in the health care issue.

1. The Rise of Premium Medicine

Here are five key points to consider:

- Over the past 30 years in the United States, the practice of medicine has become more expensive. Compared with the past, today's medical care might be termed "premium medicine."

- Premium medicine utilizes both more physical capital (such as MRI machines) and human capital (specialists).

- Premium medicine reflects cultural expectations that call for a high level of effort to diagnose ailments correctly and treat them effectively.

- Premium medicine clearly has increased the cost of health care. The evidence on whether it has increased the benefits of health care is mixed.

- Because we have conquered many infectious diseases, to increase longevity further we must tackle degenerative diseases, the treatment of which brings less bang for the buck in terms of life extension. This will reinforce the trend toward more visible cost increases and less visible benefit increases.

On April 11, 2005, a Weblogger writing under the pseudonym Quixote published a long, dramatic account of her experience of obtaining treatment for an inflammation around her eye. She vividly described her ensuing odyssey, from the opening trip to an emergency room through her frustration with her expenses and with private health insurance. Her story seems to touch on every aspect of our health care system, from hospital food to emergency services. The sidebar excerpts only those parts that deal with actual attempts to diagnose and treat her ailment.

7

Treating Eye Inflammation: A Patient's Story

The trouble started innocently enough. I had something in my eye, so I rubbed it. As any mother or eye doctor can tell you, that didn't help. Three days later my left eye was swelling visibly and growing more painful by the hour. . . . At eight thirty in the morning, my partner, Paul, drove me to the emergency room. . . . At eleven, I was trundled off for a CAT scan. . . . The doctor decided my case needed input from a specialist. . . . When the [ear, nose, and throat] doctor arrived, he. . .referred me to an eye specialist at the Dean McGee Eye Institute. . . . The doctor gave me an IV dose of broad-spectrum antibiotics, just in case the swelling was caused by infection, and told us to get to the hospital immediately. . . . We arrived at the emergency entrance to one of the big local hospitals at one thirty . . . [first-year resident] Dr. Murphy took a history of the condition, did a number of tests, and then couldn't manage to measure my intraocular pressure . . . [so he] called in a third-year resident. The new doctor went over the diagnostic data, looked at my horrific eye, and both doctors decided they needed to confer with the orbital tissues specialist. . . . Dr. Murphy had ordered the strongest stuff known to science, vancomycin, in the fear that I might have a drug-resistant infection. . . . When the doctor came, it turned out I was to go to the Eye Institute itself for my eye exam. Apparently, I was an "interesting case" and there would be several doctors. There were. The small examining room filled up with white coats. . . . The next day I woke feeling much better. The pain was noticeably reduced, although the swelling was down only slightly. Dr. Sigler still didn't approve, ordered another CAT scan, and started me on IV corticosteroids.[1]

My guess is that 30 years ago, a patient with similar symptoms would have been treated "empirically," a term doctors use to describe a situation for which they do not have a precise diagnosis and treatment, so that instead they must use guesswork. A layman's synonym for treated empirically would be "trial and error." In this case, the patient might have been sent home with an antibiotic and perhaps a prescription for Prednisone, a steroid used to reduce inflammation. There would have been nothing else to do. In 1975, computerized medical imaging technology was new and exotic, with limited applications.

In contrast, in 2005, over the course of a few days Quixote was given a computed tomography (CT) scan, referred to a specialist, sent to a different hospital, referred to a specialty clinic, seen by a battery of specialists there, and given yet another CT scan. Ultimately, however, she was sent home, as she might have been 30 years ago, with an antibiotic, Prednisone, and no firm diagnosis.

Compared with 30 years ago, Quixote received more services, in the form of specialist consultations and high-tech diagnostics. However, the ultimate treatment and outcome were no different.

This does not mean that medicine is no better today than it was a generation ago. The CT scans and specialist consultations *could* have turned out differently. They *might* have been critically important, depending on her actual condition. Under some circumstances, treating Quixote empirically with an antibiotic and Prednisone *could* have been a mistake, perhaps costing some or all of her sight in one eye.

Such is modern medicine in the United States. Doctors are able to take extra precautions. They can use more specialized knowledge and better technology to try to pin down the diagnosis. They can perform tests to rule out improbable but dangerous conditions. But only in a minority of cases does the outcome deviate from what would have been the case 30 years ago.

Figure 1-1 shows the growth in specialized medicine from 1975 to 2002. Over this period, the total population of the United States rose by 35 percent. Meanwhile, the total number of active physicians more than doubled, even though the number of general practitioners only increased by 55 percent, slightly more than the rate of increase in the population.[2]

The United States has perhaps the highest ratio of specialists to general practitioners in the industrial world. However, in aggregate data, it is very difficult to find a significant effect of specialist supply on health care outcomes.[3]

The United States also tends to be an outlier in its use of expensive medical procedures. Heart bypass surgery is about three times as prevalent here as in France and about twice as prevalent as in the

Figure 1-1
PERCENTAGE INCREASE IN NUMBER OF PHYSICIANS BY SPECIALTY,
1975–2002

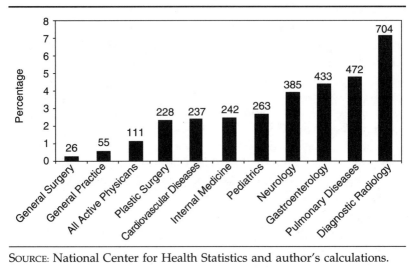

SOURCE: National Center for Health Statistics and author's calculations.

U.K. Angioplasty is more than twice as prevalent here as in France and about seven times as prevalent as in the U.K.[4]

Specialization represents the human capital component of premium medicine. The other component is physical capital, particularly diagnostic imaging technology. Todd A. Gould points out that "As late as 1982, there were but a handful of MRI scanners in the entire United States. Today there are thousands. We can image in seconds what used to take hours."[5]

According to the marketing consulting firm IMV, more than 24 million MRI exams were conducted in 2003, and more than 50 million CT scans were performed in the same year.[6] Each represents a 10 percent increase from 2002. Combining this information with data from radiology researcher Dr. Fred A. Mettler and colleagues provides the following graph for the growth of high-tech diagnostic imaging in the United States (see Figure 1-2).[7]

In March 2005, Mark Miller, Executive Director of the Medicare Payment Advisory Commission, testified that "Diagnostic imaging services paid under Medicare's physician fee schedule grew more rapidly than any other type of physician service between 1999 and

Figure 1-2
GROWTH OF CT AND MRI SCANS IN THE UNITED STATES,
1980–2003

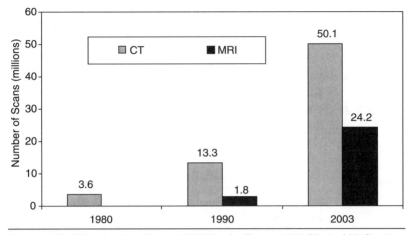

SOURCES: Gail Prochaska, "Latest IMV Study Shows MRI Clinical Utilization Expanding," *IMV, Limited*, April 19, 2005; Gail Prochaska,"Latest IMV CT Census Confirms That CT Is the Workhorse of Radiology," *IMV, Limited*, February 4, 2005; F. A. Mettler Jr. et al., "Use of Radiology in U.S. General Short-Term Hospitals: 1980–1990," *Radiology* 189 (1993): 377–380.

2003. While the sum of all physician services grew 22 percent in those years, imaging services grew twice as fast, by 45 percent."[8] More detailed breakdowns showed that "Spending for MRI, CT, and nuclear medicine has grown faster than for other imaging services. Thus, these categories represent an increasing share of total imaging spending. MRI spending grew by 116 percent between 1999 and 2003, nuclear medicine by 104 percent, and CT by 84 percent."[9] Miller's testimony noted that there is wide variation in the usage rate of diagnostic imaging service across regions, but it is difficult to find a relationship between health outcomes and usage rates.

American Cultural Expectations

The term "premium medicine" is meant to describe this heavy usage of specialist consultations and advanced medical technology. I believe that it embodies American cultural considerations, including

11

our can-do spirit, our high expectations as health care consumers, and the high standards to which doctors hold themselves.

The cliché of 30 years ago was "Take two aspirin and call me in the morning." Today, the wait-and-see approach is going the way of the house call. Instead, premium medicine looks for ways to determine the causes of ailments, bring immediate relief, and eliminate risks.

An important characteristic of premium medicine is that many procedures have a low probability of affecting the outcome. In fact, often the procedures do not even affect the treatment plan.

Consider three options for treatment:

- Do nothing.
- Treat empirically.
- Treat on the basis of a thorough diagnosis, ruling out minor possibilities.

The first option is what was meant by "take two aspirin and call me in the morning." In fact, ailments often get better if they run their course. At the other end of the scale, a terminal ailment's progress may be such that no treatment can avert the outcome. The intermediate cases are ones in which treatment might make a difference.

The second option is one a general practitioner follows on the basis of instinct and experience. Having seen similar cases before, the doctor proposes the treatment plan based on what worked in the past and the patient's characteristics.

The third option incorporates premium medicine. Biomedical tests, diagnostic imaging, and specialist consultations are included in the process of determining a treatment plan.

Consider a sample of 1,000 patients who have a severe cough that seems to be a bronchial infection. If the option chosen is "do nothing," suppose that 800 will get better and 200 will develop severe infections. If the option chosen is to "treat empirically" with an antibiotic, suppose that 998 will get better and only two patients will fail to recover. If the option chosen is to obtain a chest X-ray, suppose that all 1,000 patients will be given the correct treatment.

In this hypothetical example, the chest X-ray represents premium medicine. It would raise the cost for each of the 1,000 patients. However, the chest X-ray would change the course of treatment for only two of those 1,000 patients. Thus, the probability that premium medicine will affect the outcome in our example is only .002, or two-tenths of 1 percent.

Thus, although the costs are widespread and visible, the benefits are concentrated and hard to spot when diluted by the entire population. In particular, the benefits are unlikely to show up in aggregate statistics on health care, such as national average longevity.

Abundance and Premium Medicine

Premium medicine includes

- Routine screening procedures such as colonoscopies for people over age 50 or with a family history of colon cancer.
- MRIs and CT scans that are performed for the purpose of ruling out unlikely causes of symptoms (e.g., an MRI for someone complaining of lower back pain).
- "Heroic" efforts at late-stage treatment that usually fail but occasionally succeed.

The conditions that have given rise to premium medicine include

- Abundant medical resources, particularly the availability of specialists and advanced medical technology.
- High expectations on the part of patients.
- Strong desire on the part of doctors to meet impossibly high expectations.
- Fear of the consequences of not following premium procedures, in part because of malpractice litigation.[10]
- The belief that for patients with insurance, no consideration needs to be given to cost.

In short, there is a cultural component to premium medicine. Resource availability, high expectations, and third-party payments all provide support for premium medicine.

13

If premium medicine is the main reason that U.S. health care spending is higher than that of other countries, then an attempt to restrain health care spending by copying other countries' government-paid health care systems could backfire. For example, suppose that we treat as given our cultural attitudes toward medical care, with our bias toward taking extra precautions and undertaking more procedures whenever patients are not paying out-of-pocket. If we then layer onto this culture a system of government financing for all health care, spending would only increase beyond what we observe today.

One of the characteristics of premium medicine is that there is considerable regional variation in medical procedures, even controlling for patient characteristics. This variation has been found among the Medicare population, which is yet another indication that habits and culture are important determinants of (over-)utilization of medical services.

Instead of government financing, the crisis of abundance may require a different policy prescription. If premium medicine is to be socially beneficial, then doctors and patients must be highly cognizant of costs and benefits. Government may promote research and education concerning probabilities and outcomes from various procedures. Financial reforms, however, should move more in the direction of providing patients the incentives to use medical care wisely, rather than in the direction of further insulating patients from costs.

Evidence for the Prevalence of Premium Medicine

According to a report on trends in health care utilization in the United States, in 2000 the number of office visits to specialists per 1,000 in the population was more than 1,400—very close to the number of office visits to primary care physicians (general practitioners, internists, and pediatricians).[11] This occurred despite the fact that part of the focus of managed care in the 1990s was on reducing the utilization of specialists relative to primary care physicians.

The work of John Wennberg, Elliot Fisher, and Jonathan Skinner seems to confirm the prevalence of premium medicine.[12] They found large variations across hospital referral regions (e.g., Minneapolis vs. Miami) in the amount of Medicare expenditures in the last six months of life, with no visible variation in survival rates. Dartmouth professor John Wennberg summarized research on variation in medical care in a lecture.[13] Wennberg emphasized the importance of what he termed "preference-sensitive" care and "supply-sensitive" care.

Discussions of health care policy frequently speak of all health care as a necessity. However, Wennberg emphasizes that health care services are highly diverse and that many aspects of health care are indeed discretionary.

What we would think of as necessary care, Wennberg terms "effective care." Effective care is the care that a physician or hospital would supply if best practices were being followed. Wennberg cites the use of beta-blockers following heart attacks as an example of an effective treatment that is frequently not utilized.

Preference-sensitive care is Wennberg's term for treatment that is a matter of choice, such as lumpectomy vs. mastectomy for breast cancer. His view of the research is that preference-sensitive care often reflects the preferences of physicians rather than the preferences of patients. In many instances, Wennberg suggests, patients actually would prefer more conservative, less expensive approaches.

Finally, Wennberg argues that much care, particularly in the latter stages of life, is supply-sensitive. After heart surgery, how often should you see a cardiologist? It turns out that this is determined not by some established medical protocol but by the availability of office hours. Where there are more cardiologists per patient, follow-up visits tend to be scheduled more frequently.

Wennberg writes, "Medical theories and medical evidence play little role in governing the frequency of use of supply-sensitive services. For patients at a given stage in the progression of chronic illness, medical textbooks contain no evidence-based clinical guidelines for scheduling patients for return visits, when to hospitalize or admit to intensive care, when to refer to a medical specialist, and, for most conditions, when to order a diagnostic or imaging test."[14]

The often heavy reliance on diagnostic procedures, consultations, hospitalizations, and specialist referrals provides some evidence that premium medicine is responsible for America's high levels of health spending.

Availability of Colonoscopy Screening

Other countries appear to be less aggressive than the United States in adopting premium medicine. For example, the United States is the only country where colonoscopies are commonly used to screen for colon cancer. In the *Journal of the National Cancer Institute* (U.K.), Renee Twombly wrote:

> In the United States, people age 50 or older have the "luxury" of deciding among colonoscopy, flexible sigmoidoscopy, fecal occult blood test (FOBT), and other tests for colon cancer screening. But for many others around the world, such screening—not to mention a choice in tests—is not part of their health care routine even though colorectal cancer is one of the top cancer killers.

> Years after the discovery that colorectal screening can decrease cancer incidence and deaths, few countries have adopted widespread colon cancer screening programs, although some are inching their way to that goal.

> The reason, say many experts, is the burden that extensive colon cancer screening places on colonoscopy services. Behind every colorectal screening test, no matter what kind, is the potential need for a colonoscopy. If results from an FOBT, a barium enema, or even a flexible sigmoidoscopy to examine the lower colon are positive, patients must be referred for a colonoscopy that can view the entire colon and remove precancerous polyps, if need be. But many countries cannot yet fulfill that need, and such recommendations have huge implications for countries with national health care systems such as Canada and the United Kingdom.

Twombly quotes Desmond Leddin, head of the Division of Gastroenterology at Dalhousie University in Halifax, Nova Scotia:

> Whereas the United States has one gastroenterologist per 30,000 people, Canada has one per 100,000. . . . How are we going to provide all those services, which involves not just gastroenterologists, but pathologists, radiologists, genetics counselors, surgeons, beds, and so on? I can't get the government to fund even high-risk patients.[15]

Looking Ahead

As longevity improves and medical science continues to develop, the growth of premium medicine will present even greater challenges.

In his book *Genome*, science journalist Matt Ridley has a chapter called "Immortality" in which he describes cell regeneration in humans:

> Every time the chromosome is copied, a little bit of the telomere is left off. After a few hundred copyings, the chromosome is getting so short at the end that meaningful genes are in danger of being left off. . . . That is why cells grow old and cease to thrive beyond a certain age.[16]

What I take from this is that age-related cell death may take many forms, depending on how the chromosome is damaged by old age. But unless we can fundamentally slow the cell-aging process, we will not be able to extend the life span beyond a certain maximum.

Consider two paradigms for trying to extend longevity. One paradigm is to work on cures for specific diseases. An alternative paradigm, proposed by biogerontologist Aubrey de Grey, is to focus on trying in a fundamental way to stop cell decay.[17]

The disease-fighting paradigm contributed to the increase in life span thus far. Reducing deaths from infectious diseases reduced mortality early in life and perhaps also made people less susceptible to cancer and heart disease in middle age. In the latter part of the 20th century, measured longevity in the United States increased fairly steadily. Each decade, life span increased by about 2.5 years.[18]

However, the marginal cost of life extension is probably increasing. The disease-fighting paradigm necessarily faces a steep curve of diminishing returns: the better we get at curing infectious diseases, the more likely it is that debilitating diseases will catch up with us. We prevent heart attacks, but we succumb to cancer. We cure some cancers, but then more of us die of Alzheimer's disease. And so on.

Collectively, the debilitating diseases represent an impossible obstacle today. If the only disease likely to kill you before age 40 is an infectious disease, then curing infectious diseases buys a lot of life extension. However, there is no easy way to add 40 years to the life span of 80-year-olds. There are too many debilitating diseases for which we would have to discover and implement cures. That reality is what convinces me that, under our current paradigm, we face diminishing returns in terms of life extension.

Assuming that we continue to follow the disease-fighting paradigm, each additional year of life will be bought more dearly. If so, then the cost of premium medicine will rise further, its benefits will be more uncertain, and the financial challenges that it poses will become even more significant.

2. Three Health Care Narratives

Among economists, there are generally three major competing narratives concerning what ails health care finance in America. Although these narratives are not mutually exclusive, as a practical matter individual economists who favor one narrative tend to discount the others.

- Private health insurance does not work.
- Health care providers overcharge for their services.
- Premium medicine accounts for most of the rise in health care costs.

I find the premium medicine narrative most persuasive. This chapter looks at the strengths and weaknesses of the alternative narratives.

It turns out that for each narrative, there is a potential solution in the form of a single-payer health plan. However, the three solutions differ from one another. This suggests that "single-payer" may have multiple meanings.

Private Insurance Failure

The narrative of private insurance failure says that health insurance will not work because risk pools will break down. People who believe that they are healthy will tend to avoid insurance. People who suspect that they are likely to need health care will gravitate toward insurance, but that will cause premiums to be high, making it even more likely that healthy people will choose to avoid health insurance. This process is described by Tim Harford in *The Undercover Economist*:

> The insurance company only sells insurance to people who are confident they will use it. As a result, the insurer loses clients who are unlikely to make claims and acquires the unwanted clients who are likely to make costly claims, and then the insurer has to cut back on benefits and raise premiums. . . . More and more people cancel their policies.[1]

According to this narrative, a major reason that health insurance is expensive is that health insurance companies devote considerable resources to deal with the problem of adverse selection. No company wants to be the insurer of choice for sick people, so it has to put effort into designing and administering plans in such a way that it excludes the sickest people from coverage.

This narrative suggests that the main reason there are people without health insurance is that the risk pool has broken down. People who believe that they are healthy will opt out of insurance. People who are particularly sick will be rejected by insurance companies.

What I question about this narrative is its practical significance. Although private health insurance markets *could* break down because of risk pooling failures, there is not much direct evidence that they *do* break down in that way. Employer-provided health insurance, which is the basis for much of the private health insurance in this country, tends to mitigate the potential for adverse selection. Moreover, even in the individual insurance market, the evidence suggests that health insurance companies are able to pool risks effectively.[2]

Another question about the theory of pooling breaking down is: why now? If private insurance is inherently unworkable, then it should have been unworkable in 1955 and in 1975. However, the growing population of uninsured and the unraveling of employer-provided health insurance are relatively recent phenomena.

It is difficult to argue that private health insurance *per se* is the reason that health care costs are high in the United States. As a line item of our national health care accounts, health insurance administration accounts for about 1 percent of GDP, out of total health care spending of 15 percent of GDP.

For those who believe this narrative, the most awkward fact to deal with is that Medicare fails to demonstrate an ability to hold down health care costs. The argument that government-provided health insurance reduces health care costs or that Medicare is more efficient than private health insurance is not supported by international comparisons of spending by age category.

Consider the four populations in Table 2-1: The group that is unique in its heavy reliance on private health insurance is the first group, Americans under age 65. In the United States, the private sector accounts for a much larger share of health care spending for people under age 65 than is the case in other OECD countries. For

Table 2-1
SOURCES OF HEALTH INSURANCE, ELDERLY AND NONELDERLY,
U.S. VS. EUROPE

Population Group	Main Source of Insurance
Americans under age 65	Private
Europeans under age 65	Public
Americans over age 65	Public
Europeans over age 65	Public

people over age 65, the proportion of spending paid for by the U.S. government is comparable to that in other countries.

In principle, if government were more efficient in financing health care, then spending on patients in government programs would more closely track those patients' needs than would private-sector spending. Consider the ratio of health care spending on the elderly to health care spending on the nonelderly. Theoretically, in countries with government-financed health care, this ratio should reflect the difference in needs between the two populations. However, in the United States, this ratio is affected by the fact that health care for the nonelderly population has a much larger private component. If Medicare were more efficient than private health insurance, and if privately funded health care spending were the reason that the United States spends more on health care, then the ratio of spending on the elderly to spending on the nonelderly should be lower in the United States.

Looking at the ratio of per capita spending on the elderly to per capita spending on the nonelderly, the United States is not an outlier among OECD countries. Although the U.S. ratio is lower than that of some countries, it is higher than the ratios in other countries where government-provided health care is more widespread. In Canada, the level of per capita health care spending on people age 65 and older is 5.4 times that spent on people under age 65. That ratio is 4.9 in Japan, 4.0 in the United States, and 3.4 in the United Kingdom.[3]

The "natural experiment" of using Medicare to pay for health care for those over age 65 in the United States does not reduce the overall cost of health care for that group. What this natural experiment suggests is that America's high rate of health care spending reflects our culture and the abundance of resources. Our higher rate of spending holds for people over age 65, where government is heavily involved, as well as for people under age 65, where government is much less involved.

That observation is consistent with the view that differences in medical practices rather than differences in financing systems are what account for the differences in health care spending. Premium medicine is practiced in the United States for all age groups, for those insured both privately and by government. It is the extensive use of premium medicine that makes health care spending higher in the United States than in other countries.

Providers Overcharge

The narrative of health care providers overcharging for services is represented by the slogan, "It's the Prices, Stupid," which was the title of a prominent article written by Gerard Anderson and other health policy scholars. That article's thesis is that America's health care costs are due mostly to the high incomes earned by service providers.[4]

According to this narrative, the parties that pay for health care services are at the mercy of doctors, hospitals, and medical equipment makers. The purchasers are fragmented, and they lack bargaining power. Suppliers earn above-normal profits and incomes, and health care is inordinately expensive. Consumers suffer either directly, because health insurance is expensive, or indirectly, as they forgo wages to obtain employer-based health coverage or pony up taxes to pay for government-provided health insurance.

Anderson and his coauthors do not focus a great deal on direct measurement of prices. That is, they do not compare the price of, say, an office visit to a dermatologist in the United States with an office visit to a dermatologist in France. Instead, they rely primarily on data that show total expenditures are higher in the United States. To suggest that this is due to price rather than quality of services, they point to cross-country indicators such as average longevity, in which the United States clearly does no better than countries that spend much less per person on health care.

Anderson and colleagues are suggesting indirectly that the U.S. health care system provides no more in medical services than are provided by other industrialized countries. However, the direct evidence suggests that rising U.S. health care expenditures reflect more than just price increases. In 1980, the share of U.S. GDP devoted to health care was comparable to the share in other OECD countries. Only in the last 25 years has the share of GDP that we devote to health care become a significant outlier. In that period, although health care prices have risen faster than inflation, per capita consumption of real health care services (that is, the value of health care measured in constant dollars, adjusted for higher health care prices) has gone up at least as fast as the relative price of health care services.

What the National Income Accounts Tell Us

In 1980, the U.S. national income accounts showed that personal health care expenditures were $214.6 billion. In 2003, personal health care expenditures were $1,440.8 billion.[5]

The ratio of spending in 2003 to spending in 1980 was 6.71, which means that we spent almost seven times as much in 2003. Arithmetically, this ratio can be decomposed as follows:

$$\frac{\substack{\textit{Health}\\\textit{Spending}\\\textit{in 2003}}}{\substack{\textit{Health}\\\textit{Spending}\\\textit{in 1980}}} = \frac{\substack{\textit{Population}\\\textit{in 2003}}}{\substack{\textit{Population}\\\textit{in 1980}}} \times \frac{\substack{\textit{Real Per Capita}\\\textit{Services in}\\\textit{2003}}}{\substack{\textit{Real Per Capita}\\\textit{Services in}\\\textit{1980}}} \times \frac{\substack{\textit{General Price}\\\textit{Level in}\\\textit{2003}}}{\substack{\textit{General Price}\\\textit{Level in}\\\textit{1980}}} \times \frac{\substack{\textit{Relative Price of}\\\textit{Health Care}\\\textit{in 2003}}}{\substack{\textit{Relative Price of}\\\textit{Health Care}\\\textit{in 1980}}}$$

Inserting the values in Table 2-2 gives us

$$\frac{\$1{,}440.8 \text{ billion}}{\$214.6 \text{ billion}} = \frac{296.1 \text{ million}}{230.4 \text{ million}} \times \frac{\$4{,}352}{\$2{,}708} \times \frac{106}{54} \times \frac{111.8/106}{34.4/54}$$

Which reduces to

$$6.71 \quad \approx \quad 1.29 \quad \times \quad 1.61 \quad \times \quad 1.96 \quad \times \quad 1.66$$

The relative price of health care is the GDP deflator for health care services divided by the overall GDP deflator, a measure of overall inflation. It represents the national income accounts measure of the contribution of rising health care prices to health care spending. Table 2-2 shows in another format how the increase in spending between 1980 and 2003 breaks down.

Table 2-2
CONTRIBUTORS TO GROWTH IN U.S. HEALTH CARE
SPENDING, 1980–2003

Category	1980	2003	Ratio of 2003 to 1980
Total Personal Health Care Spending	$214.6 billion	$1,440.8 billion	6.71
Population	230.4 million	296.1 million	1.29
Real Per Capita Spending	$2,708	$4,352	1.61
General Price Level	54	106	1.96
Relative Price of Health Care	34.4/54	111.8/106	1.66

SOURCE: Cynthia Smith et al., "Health Spending Growth Slows in 2003," *Health Affairs* 24, No. 1, Jan.–Feb. 2005, pp. 185–194. Author's calculations.

The relative price of health care, as measured in the national income accounts, certainly rose dramatically between 1980 and 2003.[6] However, it by no means accounts for all of the increase in personal health care spending over that period. Together, the increase in population and the increase in real per capita spending were slightly more important as a driver of total health care spending. That is, the increase in total health services consumed was slightly larger than the increase in the relative cost of health care services.

Perhaps the most important line to focus on in Table 2-2 is real (inflation-adjusted) per capita spending on health care. The fact that it was 1.61 times higher in 2003 than in 1980 means that the average American consumed 60 percent more services in 2003 than in 1980.

As noted in Chapter 1, "The Rise of Premium Medicine," direct measures of health care supply, such as the number of medical specialists and the use of computer-assisted imaging services, show dramatic increases over the past three decades. This direct evidence suggests that Americans are consuming a mix of services that has a high intensity of both physical and human capital.

The most awkward fact for the narrative that attributes high health care spending solely to prices is the finding by John Wennberg and his colleagues that health care utilization differs sharply by region within the United States. Using comparable populations, Wennberg and others have shown that there are differences in spending within the United States that are comparable to the differences in spending that we observe between the United States and other countries. Just as with the international data, there is a tendency to find little or no difference in health care outcomes between high-spending and low-spending regions. However, by looking directly at utilization figures, it is clear that when it comes to explaining spending differences across regions it is not the prices. Patients in high-spending regions see more physicians and undergo more procedures than patients in low-spending regions.[7]

Premium Medicine

The premium medicine narrative discussed in Chapter 1 states that high health care costs are due to greater use of specialists and advanced technology. That in turn raises the cost of health insurance, which pays for such capital-intensive medical care.

The most awkward fact for the premium medicine narrative is that health care outcomes, as measured by national average longevity or age-adjusted mortality, are no better on average in the United States than in other countries. If our high levels of health care spending are the result of so-called premium medicine, we should be demonstrably healthier. Yet when we attempt to examine average longevity at a national level, there seems to be no connection between America's high levels of health care spending and life span.

What might explain these findings? I suggest the following factors. First, at the margin, the differences in average longevity that one would expect to find from health care spending are small. Second, aggregate longevity is affected by deaths in which medical intervention would make no difference (e.g., homicides and traffic fatalities), by behavioral factors (e.g., smoking and nutrition), and by circumstances at birth and early childhood (e.g., genetic factors), regardless of subsequent health care.

Looking for Small Differences

The United States spends about $5,000 per capita on health care, while other major OECD countries spend about $3,000 per capita. In percentage or aggregate terms, the difference is enormous, but the dollar difference per person amounts to just $2,000.

David Cutler estimates that the value of a life-year is $100,000. If the additional $2,000 that we spend on health care were just cost-effective, then it would increase longevity by 2/100 of a year ($2,000 divided by $100,000), or about one week. That is, each year of additional spending at a rate of $2,000 a year should add about one week to longevity. Even if we spent at this rate for 20 years, the cumulative effect should be less than one-half of one year. That partly explains why premium medicine does not seem to increase longevity.

The effect of health care spending on longevity is dissipated further by the fact that some medical treatments are dedicated solely to relief from suffering. From a longevity perspective, every dollar spent on relief from allergy symptoms, pain, depression, disability, or discomfort is "wasted."

Nonmedical Factors

If aggregate longevity were measured precisely and reflected nothing other than health care, then it could be a valuable indicator, even if we were looking for small differences. However, there are many factors apart from health care that affect longevity. In fact, for young people, whose death rates exert a heavy influence on average national longevity, health care is far from the most important factor.

One measure that relates closely to longevity is life-years lost before age 75. In a given year, one multiplies the number of people who die at each age by the difference between 75 and the age of death. The measure is standardized by looking at life-years lost per 100,000 people. In the United States in 2002, the number of life-years lost per 100,000 people was 7,500. Of this, 1,700 life-years, or more than 20 percent, were lost due to deaths from accidents, suicides, and homicides.[8]

Behavioral and environmental factors also affect longevity. Death from heart disease has declined dramatically in the United States over the past 50 years. In fact, the drop is more than might be accounted for by the use of interventions such as open heart surgeries. Cleaner air, easier working conditions, and earlier retirement are among the nonmedical factors that have contributed to the reduced rate of mortality from heart disease.

Within the United States, there are significant variations in longevity by region and by social class. These differences exist within other countries as well. In *Genome*, Matt Ridley notes that a study found that "British civil servants working in Whitehall also get heart disease in proportion to their lowliness in the bureaucratic pecking order . . . the status of a person's job was more able to predict their likelihood of a heart attack than obesity, smoking or high blood pressure."[9]

With all of these factors affecting longevity, it seems brave to read much into differences in national averages. The number and importance of nonmedical factors seem staggering.

Genetic and Birth Factors

There is strong evidence that both genetic factors and health conditions at birth affect longevity. Immigrants tend to share the longevity of their ethnic origin, rather than automatically acquiring the longevity of their new country. This should not be surprising, given that genetic factors account for differences in susceptibility to a number of diseases.

An interesting finding in longevity studies is that the month of birth affects life span. Dr. Gabriele Doblhammer-Reiter is the demographer most responsible for calling attention to this relationship:

> Differences in life span by month of birth have been shown to exist in Australia, Austria, Denmark, and the United States. For Australia the month-of-birth pattern is shifted by half a year, compared with the Northern Hemisphere. The peak-to-trough differences range between 0.41 years in Denmark and 0.73 years in Austria. Among migrants, the month-of-birth pattern resembles the pattern of their place of birth rather than of their residence. A comparison of the month-of-birth patterns in infant mortality between 1911 and 1915 and mortality at ages 50 plus shows they are highly positively correlated. The spring-born have a higher mortality risk during their first year of life and after age 50.[10]

An implication of the long duration of the month-of-birth effect is that there probably are other conditions at birth that have even stronger and equally durable effects. Indeed, in the September 17,

2004, issue of *Science*, gerontologists Caleb Finch and Eileen Crimmins published a study showing that early exposure to infectious diseases increases the risk of heart attack, stroke, and cancer years later.[11] One implication of their work is that the longevity that we measure among the elderly today reflects in part the conditions they experienced in the 1920s and 1930s.

Overall, I believe that it is an unsettled issue whether the extra dollars that the United States spends on health care lead to better results and, if so, whether the difference is sufficient to justify the costs. In light of the work by Wennberg and colleagues on regional differences in health care spending, it may be that trying to show a relationship between health care spending and outcomes is an uphill battle. However, I would not take international comparisons of longevity as a definitive indication that all of the additional expenditure by the U.S. health care system is wasted.

Insurance and the Three Narratives

The three narratives reach different conclusions about the role of America's health insurance system in health care costs. The insurance-failure narrative says that private health insurance, with its inherent susceptibility to adverse selection, is itself the source of high costs in health care. The supplier-overpricing narrative says that private insurance fails to exert enough discipline to hold supplier incomes below exorbitant levels. The premium medicine narrative says that what we call health insurance is not really insurance, and that it contributes to higher spending by reducing the incentive of consumers and doctors to take cost into account when making decisions.

Single-Payer, Multiple Solutions

One could advocate a single-payer health care system, with the government as the sole financer of health care, regardless of which of the three narratives one finds most persuasive. However, these would not be identical single-payer systems. The systems that go along with each narrative are described in Table 2-3.

The doctor-friendly approach to a single-payer health care system would be based on a fee-for-service approach, where suppliers determine the normal fee. Government would not be involved in deciding which services are appropriate for payment or which price is set for

Table 2-3
DIFFERENT EXPLANATIONS OF AMERICA'S HEALTH CARE
FINANCING "CRISIS" AND DIFFERENT APPROACHES TO SINGLE-
PAYER HEALTH CARE

Narrative	Single-Payer Approach	Description
Insurance failure	Doctor-friendly	Reimburses doctors at usual rates
Supplier overpricing	Doctor-hostile	Reimburses doctors at lower rates
Premium medicine	Doctor-limiting	Rations the supply and/or use of health care providers

doctors. Government's sole role would be administrative, to collect taxes and pay medical claims. Given the narrative that private insurance market failure is the problem with the health care system, the government should be able to reduce health care costs through administrative savings.

The doctor-hostile approach would have the government crack down on supplier incomes. Government would act as a tough bargaining agent with doctors and hospitals. Given the narrative that suppliers are guilty of overpricing, the government should be able to reduce health care costs by requiring doctors and hospitals to accept lower reimbursement rates.

A doctor-limiting approach would impose a national health care budget. Doctors would not have discretion over the treatment plan for a patient. Instead, procedures would not be paid for if the administrative bureaucracy determines they are not cost-effective. Given the narrative of premium medicine, which suggests that patients undergo expensive procedures with low expected benefits, health care rationing presumably could restrain spending without worsening outcomes.

In practice, a single-payer system would be tugged back and forth among these three models, just as Medicare is tugged back and forth today. Physicians prefer the doctor-friendly model. However, to restrain costs, government tries to reimburse doctors at lower rates, with the result that some doctors refuse to handle Medicare patients. By setting conditions for reimbursement, government also sets limits on the discretion of physicians.

Because I view premium medicine as the most plausible narrative, my prediction would be that neither the doctor-friendly nor doctor-hostile approaches to single-payer health care would work. By insulating the consumer from health care costs, a single-payer system would not offer any incentive for consumers to ration their own health care spending, and in an environment of premium medicine that can only lead to skyrocketing expenditures. In the end, I think that single-payer would have to resort to severe centralized health care rationing.

In fact, any health care system that we adopt—and I believe that we will always have a mixed system that includes expenses paid for by government, by private insurance, and out-of-pocket—will be subject to the competing pressures of patients' and physicians' desire for autonomy, the patient's desire to be insulated from cost, and society's need to restrain health care spending. However, an alternative to centralized rationing is to have *individuals* undertake rationing decisions, by comparing costs and benefits. That means raising the share of out-of-pocket spending, an approach described in Chapter 6, "Matching Funding Systems to Needs." Government may have a role in assembling and disseminating information that helps individuals make choices about health care procedures. That will be discussed further in Chapter 8, "Policy Ideas."

Other Narratives

Before moving on, I should mention a few other narratives for our health care system. I do not believe that these narratives are as plausible as the three main narratives already discussed.

One narrative is that high drug company profits are a major cause of high health care costs. Another narrative is that malpractice insurance premiums are a large factor. Still another narrative is that people without health insurance "free ride" by obtaining health care on an emergency basis, with the cost borne by taxpayers or by higher prices set for insured patients. However, neither drug company profits nor malpractice costs nor "free riding" amounts to even one-half of 1 percent of GDP, when total health care spending is 15 percent of GDP. Malpractice litigation probably exacerbates the use of premium medicine by encouraging defensive medicine. However, I suspect that other cultural factors are the significant causes of our intensive use of specialist referrals and advanced equipment.

George Mason University economist Robin Hanson offers another narrative. Health services are a way of showing the sick that we care about them, but on average they are not an effective way of improving the outcome because harmful care roughly cancels out helpful care at the margin. He suggests that this narrative best explains the many studies that seem to show little difference in outcomes among different populations despite differences in expenditure.[12]

3. Dollars and Decisions

Here are five key points to consider:

- Many health care services are neither absolutely necessary nor absolutely unnecessary. Instead, they fall in a gray area where costs and benefits need to be weighed carefully.
- Cost-benefit analysis of medical protocols is difficult. The benefits of many types of health care are probabilistic. The results of a diagnostic procedure or a treatment cannot be known in advance.
- Many medical procedures, particularly diagnostic imaging, are performed with a low probability of making a major difference in the ultimate outcome. The occasional benefits are diluted in the average population by the large number of cases in which the procedure turns out not to matter.
- Cost-benefit analysis is further complicated by the possibility of multiple medical protocols. A protocol may appear to be cost-effective compared with doing nothing. However, when compared with an alternative protocol, it may not be cost-effective at the margin.
- Doctors frequently must make choices without access to the type of sophisticated statistical research and decision modeling that would offer the best estimate of benefits relative to costs.

The Gray Area

One potential objection to applying economics to health care is the intuition that health care is not like other goods, because demand is not sensitive to price. On the one hand, if someone needs health care, such as treatment for a heart attack or a broken arm, then it would be cruel to charge such a high price that the person cannot afford it. On the other hand, people dislike being in a hospital, so one might argue that even if hospital services were free, people would not overuse them.

The Cost of Inconvenience and Discomfort

Most people do not like to go to a doctor, undergo medical procedures, or stay in a hospital. However, economists do not see this as offsetting the tendency for people to overconsume medical services that are paid for by third parties, such as insurers, employers, or government.

To an economist, if medical services are time-consuming, inconvenient, and uncomfortable to patients, then those are real costs, and they should be factored into the decision of whether the service is worthwhile. Those costs, which might collectively be termed nonmonetary costs, should not be ignored. They belong in the equation that determines whether or not a service ought to be performed.

Suppose that the fee for a procedure is $500, and nonmonetary costs amount to the equivalent of another $1,000. If the health benefits from the service are only $750, then the service is a bad deal for the patient. The fact that the health benefits exceed the fee is interesting, but it does not justify having the patient suffer through the service.

Suppose an individual were due for a colonoscopy that would cause him or her to miss two days of work because of the preparation and recovery involved. Imagine that another procedure were available that took no time, involved no risk, and required no unpleasant preparation, but the procedure cost $100 more than a colonoscopy. Most people would opt for this alternative procedure rather than for the colonoscopy, even though from the standpoint of the insurance company the colonoscopy is "cheaper." What this hypothetical example illustrates is that nonmonetary cost is something that consumers would pay to avoid, and justifiably so.

It is possible that consumers sometimes overestimate nonmonetary costs. Perhaps people avoid going to the dentist because they believe the nonmonetary costs are high, but in the long run they would be better off if they went to the dentist. Whether people in fact overestimate nonmonetary costs is an empirical question. Perhaps at some point, research in behavioral economics will lead to an approach for estimating and adjusting for biases in subjective estimates of nonmonetary costs. However, there is no reason to believe that the right way to make health care decisions is to treat patient inconvenience and discomfort as nonexistent, thereby ignoring such costs altogether.

Table 3-1
MEDICAL CARE OF UNCERTAIN VALUE
(ASSUMING COST OF $100)

Black Region (unnecessary care)	Gray Area (unknown if benefits outweigh costs)	White Region (essential care)
The service provides $0 in benefits	Reasonable estimates of the benefits of the service range from $0 to $150	Reasonable estimates of the benefits of the service range from $150 to $10,000

On reflection, however, we see that this intuition about health care is wrong. It is *not* true that health care is a black-and-white proposition in which services are either utterly necessary or else utterly unwarranted. In fact, many services fall in what I call the "gray area." Services that fall in the gray area are services that offer some benefits but which are not absolutely necessary.

It is possible to illustrate the gray area in quantitative terms, based on the relationship between benefits and costs for a health care service. Consider Table 3-1, which offers a classification scheme for a service that costs $100: The figure of $100 is just an illustration. The boundary for the gray area should be set in the neighborhood of the actual cost of the service. If the service costs $1,000, then the boundary for the gray area might be set at around $1,200.

It is obvious that services in the black region are wasteful. It might be in the narrow self-interest of providers to bill for services in the black region, but it is not in the interest of health care consumers.

It is obvious that services in the white region ought to be performed. Treatment for a broken arm or a heart attack is sure to fall within the white region.

To know whether a service in the gray area ought to be performed, careful analysis is required. Some services have positive benefits, but those benefits are so small that resources would be better used on other things.

There is a large gray area in health care. Consider these examples:

- Suppose that a new pair of glasses offers slightly better vision and a more fashionable set of frames. The benefits are worth more than $0, but they may not be clearly worth more than the

$500 that they cost. The new pair of glasses may fall in the gray area.

- Suppose that you have a heart problem for which it is recommended that you see a cardiologist regularly, and each office visit costs $200. The annual benefits of seeing a cardiologist once a year might be well in excess of $200, and doing so would fall within the white region. But you should not see a cardiologist once a day, unless the benefits from doing so are close to $75,000 a year. Seeing a cardiologist once a week, once a month, or once a quarter also would fall under the gray area.
- A precautionary diagnostic procedure to rule out a remotely possible ailment (e.g., a routine colonoscopy to screen and prevent colon cancer) falls in the gray area. (See the discussion below.)

In theory, insurance companies and government health care financing agencies could try to manage the use of health care procedures that fall in the gray area. In practice, third-party payers face enough of a challenge in policing the black region where providers attempt to profit from services that are totally unnecessary. It is considerably more difficult for third-party payers to decline to cover procedures that offer definite positive benefits, however small.

If there were no gray area in health care, and everything were black and white, then the only policy challenge would be to make sure that people obtain the services that they need. However, the fact that there is a gray area means that there is some uncertainty about which health care services are cost-effective. That makes it important to be able to place a dollar value on the benefits of health care services.

Putting a Dollar Value on Benefits

For health care services that fall in the gray area, economists look at cost-effectiveness in terms that are not usually employed in everyday discussions of the subject. In particular, we look at

- Dollar value.
- Probability.

To make an economic decision when faced with a health care choice, one has to assign a dollar value to the possible outcomes. For example, suppose that without treatment a person will die in two years, but with treatment the person will live for 12 years. Then the benefit of treatment is 10 additional years of life. If one year of life is worth $100,000, then the value of this treatment is $1 million. In decisions where life is not at stake, the dollar value must be assigned to relief from pain, discomfort, or disability. Thus, if someone has hay fever allergies, the value of treatment is the value that the person would give not to suffer from severe sneezing, itching eyes, and other forms of discomfort.

Another factor to consider is probability. Suppose that the treatment has only a 10 percent chance of working. How does that affect the value? One mathematical approach would be to take the "expected value" of the treatment, which means multiplying the benefit of success times the probability of success. Using the example in which successful treatment saves three years of life, we multiply $300,000 times 0.1 to get an "expected value" of $30,000 for the treatment.[1]

In many cases, a treatment can reduce risk, and a diagnostic screening procedure can identify symptoms that warrant treatment. For example, suppose a person probably does not have cancer, but is deciding whether to go through a diagnostic screening (a mammogram or a colonoscopy). The procedure would detect any cancer soon enough to make it treatable, ensuring that the person will live five more years. Otherwise, suppose that the probability that a person will die from cancer in two years is one-tenth of 1 percent. Assume that person values an additional year of life at $100,000, so that if the procedure detects cancer and extends his or her life by three years, then it is worth $300,000. However, taking into account the low probability of detecting cancer, the "expected value" of this cancer screening is $300,000 times 0.001, or just $300. If some people are willing to pay more than this, that reflects a higher valuation of a year of life.

Real-World Decisions

These two factors—the value of health gains and the probability that they will occur—are implicit in every choice that we make about health care. However, they are rarely stated explicitly, and consumers almost never base their decisions on these sorts of numbers. There are challenges with estimating both factors. Some issues are subjective and some parameters are not well known.

The dollar value of improved health is somewhat subjective. For example, individuals could place different values on a year of life. At best, economists can arrive at a guess for an average value. David Cutler, a health care economist who has studied the issue, makes a case for using an approximation of $100,000 for one year of life.[2]

In contrast to our examples, in the real world the life extension that results from a successful medical procedure is not known with such certainty. A cancer treatment might be effective, but the patient could be hit by a truck. Alternatively, the treatment may extend the patient's life by many more years than the physicians expect. Because the value of the hoped-for benefits and the probability that a treatment will work are not explicitly known, it is difficult for economists to evaluate the cost-effectiveness of health care. We do not know whether or not the standard protocols are justified, although we can make rough estimates.

Low Probabilities, High Costs

In 2003, more than 24 million MRI examinations were performed in the United States. If the average cost of an MRI is $600 or more, this means that more than $14 billion was spent on MRIs. It would be interesting to know what percent of these exams resulted in a treatment plan that differed from what would have been followed without the MRI. Often, of course, the result is that "the MRI didn't turn up anything."

Suppose, for example, that if the MRI turns up a positive result, then the alteration of the treatment plan will result in a benefit that is worth $50,000 in reduced suffering to the patient. If there is a 1 percent chance that the MRI will turn up a positive result, then the "expected benefit" of the MRI is $50,000 times 0.01, or $500. If the MRI costs $600, then its "expected benefit" is less than the cost.

The point is not to single out MRIs. Many diagnostic tests and specialist referrals are undertaken to "rule out" a possibility that the internist considers unlikely. In each of these situations, the expected benefit of the procedure is diminished to the extent that the probability of a significant finding is low. The cost of the procedure may exceed its expected benefits.

Hematuria

When I was 45 years old, I had an experience that illustrates the uncertainty involved in whether or not to undertake further diagnostic procedures. During a routine physical examination, the lab that examined my urine sample found microscopic amounts of blood. This condition, known as microhematuria, can be a symptom of a number of serious illnesses, including bladder cancer.

However, the incidence of bladder cancer is very low among nonsmoking men under the age of 50. Moreover, microhematuria is present in between 10 and 15 percent of the healthy population. Finally, I had a history of occasional microhematuria, going back to my childhood. Using Bayes' Theorem (a basic probability law), I calculated that my chances of having bladder cancer were lower than that of a male age 60 *without* hematuria. Nonetheless, after much argument back and forth, my doctor insisted that I undergo a cystoscopy procedure. The results were negative.

In this case, I believe it turned out that I was correct, and that my Harvard-trained internist was in error. In a recent summary of a variety of research, Dr. Gustave Quade, of Germany's Institute of Medical Biometry, Informatics and Epidemiology, writes, "There is insufficient evidence to indicate that single hematuria testing is effective in screening for bladder cancer, and there is no evidence that single hematuria testing results in reduced mortality from the disease."[3]

Tamoxifen

Several years ago, my wife was diagnosed with early-stage breast cancer. After surgery and radiation, her five-year chances of survival were rated at 94 percent, based on statistics that were shown to us by her oncologist. The oncologist recommended that my wife take Tamoxifen, which the oncologist believed would increase my wife's survival probability to something like 96 percent. This seemed like a worthwhile increase in her chance of remaining cancer-free. Such a probabilistic justification for a treatment is quite common. Many cancer treatments serve to reduce the probability of dying from cancer, but none of them provides a sure cure.

Similarly, anti-cholesterol drugs have been shown to reduce the probability of heart attack. Still, many people who never take such drugs will be free of heart attacks and some people who do take anti-cholesterol medication will nonetheless succumb to heart disease.

Colonoscopies and Longevity, Costs and Benefits

Given all of the unknowns, the most common approach to medical decisions is to follow standard protocols, or rules of thumb. For example, a standard recommendation is that someone over age 50 should have a colonoscopy every five years to screen for colon cancer. If we looked at the probability that this approach would prevent cancer, multiplied by the number of years of life saved, then the benefits of this approach probably would exceed its service fees, although not by much.

If individuals were making the colonoscopy decision themselves, they might arrive at different choices. Someone who places a lower value on greater longevity might choose to have a colonoscopy less frequently. Someone who places a high value on more years of life might choose to have a colonoscopy more frequently. In principle, the decision should take into account a person's estimate of his or her probability of contracting a different fatal illness within the next few years.

Is Colonoscopy Screening Cost-Effective?

Consider the routine colonoscopy that is recommended every five years to screen for colon cancer for those of us over age 50. Colon cancer kills more than 50,000 people per year.[4] It seems that screening and polypectomies can prevent something like 80 percent of colon cancers.[5]

The cost-effectiveness of colonoscopy might be estimated as follows. The lifetime risk of colon cancer is 6 percent.[6] If an extension of life of five years can be obtained in 80 percent of those cases with routine colonoscopy, then the expected number of life-years saved is five times 0.06 times 0.80, or 0.24 years. If the value of a life-year is $100,000, then the expected value of routine colonoscopies is $24,000. If the protocol calls for six colonoscopies between age 50 and 75, at an average cost of $1,000 each, the total cost is $6,000. Therefore, the protocol is cost-effective.

Note, however, that the calculation could change. If the cost per procedure were $2,000 (I have been charged even more) and the value of a life-year were assumed to be $50,000, the calculation would be break-even. In that case, taking into account the nonmonetary costs of undergoing a colonoscopy, the protocol would not be cost-effective.

If colon cancer screening makes sense for people over age 50, why not for people under age 50? This raises the general question of where to draw the line for undertaking a screening or diagnostic procedure. How high does the risk have to be to justify the procedure?

Protocol A and Protocol B

In order to evaluate a screening protocol, one needs to compare alternative screening protocols. For example, using a CT scan as a "virtual colonoscopy" is an alternative to an invasive colonoscopy.[7]

A virtual colonoscopy could save nonmonetary costs in terms of time and discomfort for patients. Suppose that the total of monetary and nonmonetary cost of virtual colonoscopy is $400, and the total cost of invasive colonoscopy is $1,000. Suppose that the probability that the virtual colonoscopy will detect precancerous polyps is 80 percent (in which case invasive colonoscopy will be necessary), and the probability that invasive colonoscopy will detect precancerous polyps is 90 percent.

Suppose that we have 100,000 patients age 60, and 1 percent of them have pre-cancerous colon polyps. Consider two protocols for screening the patients to find out which ones have the polyps. Protocol A is to give 100,000 patients an invasive colonoscopy. Protocol B is to give them instead a virtual colonoscopy, only requiring an invasive colonoscopy if a polyp is detected. Here are the possible outcomes of the two protocols:

Protocol A costs $100 million ($1,000 times 100,000 patients) and finds polyps in 900 patients (90 percent of 1 percent of 100,000 patients). Protocol B costs $40 million for an initial screening ($400 times 100,000 patients), and it finds polyps in 800 patients (80 percent of 1 percent of 100,000 patients). For those 800 patients with polyps, invasive colonoscopy is required, which costs an additional $800,000. Thus, the total cost of Protocol B is $40,800,000.

Assume that Protocol A adds an average of five life-years to the 900 patients in whom it discovers polyps. The average cost per life-year saved by Protocol A is then $22,222.22 (five years times 900 lives divided by $100 million). Protocol A appears to be highly cost-effective.

So does Protocol B. It saves 4,000 life-years (800 lives times five years each) at an average cost of just $10,200 ($40,800,000 divided by 4,000 life-years).

Protocol A seems more attractive. It saves 500 more life-years than Protocol B, and does so at an average cost that is well below most people's estimation of the value of a life-year. Therefore, it is tempting to conclude that Protocol A is more desirable. However, it is important to evaluate economic choices compared with the alternatives.

If the goal is to save as many lives as possible with the money we have, then the question of whether Protocol A is cost-effective depends on whether there are alternatives that can save more lives with the same amount of money. Protocol B allows society to save 4,000 life-years at a cost of $10,200 each. By comparison, Protocol A saves an additional 500 life-years. But to save those additional life-years, society must spend a total of $59,200,000 more than it spent on Protocol B ($100 million minus $40,800,000). Therefore the actual cost of each *additional* life-year saved by Protocol A is $118,400 ($59,200,000 divided by 500 life-years). This is also called the *marginal* cost of Protocol A, because it asks, "Given what Protocol B can achieve, what additional costs and benefits does Protocol A offer?"

Assume we have decided that at the very least, we will spend $40,800,000 on colon cancer screening—enough to save 4,000 life-years through Protocol B. The question then becomes, "What is the best use of the next $59,200,000 we spend?" If spending that money on some other intervention (say, mammograms) will save 600 life-years rather than 500 life-years, then it makes sense to spend that money on mammograms.

This type of analysis demonstrates that for most medical interventions, there comes a point where the cost of saving one additional life exceeds the cost of saving a life through alternative means. At that point, it makes sense to devote any further resources to interventions that would save more lives for the money. If the goal is to save as many lives as possible with the resources we have, then this type of analysis is indispensable.

A Metaphor for International Differences?

Protocol A and Protocol B might be considered a metaphor for different health care systems. For example, in the United States, people with health insurance might be screened under Protocol A, while those without insurance might be screened under Protocol B. That is, when doctors recognize that the patient will be paying, they may be more concerned about avoiding unnecessary expense.

Protocol B also might represent health care systems in other countries. Because specialist physicians and equipment are not as prevalent in other countries, they may have to ration screening more carefully. In fact, some evidence suggests that in Canada, for example, routine mammograms and colonoscopies are not as prevalent as in the United States.[8] However, the fact that other countries restrict access to such screening does not necessarily mean that they effectively target those resources to the highest risks.

Shortage of Information

The key point of this chapter is that to make rational, cost-effective decisions on health care, doctors and patients need to take into account sophisticated and complex factors. Statistical tools like multilevel probability trees would be required to calculate the expected value of a diagnostic procedure. Marginal cost-benefit analysis is needed to determine whether a particular protocol is appropriate or overly aggressive.

We tend to discuss health care as if the choices were stark and clear. We speak as if medical procedures are always necessary and sufficient to achieve cure. In reality, treatments or diagnostic procedures typically do not produce benefits with certainty. Cost-effectiveness is affected by the probability that the patient has a particular illness, the probability that the illness will be correctly identified by the diagnostic procedure, and the probability that the treatment will alleviate the illness. Marginal cost-effectiveness is affected by the existence of alternative approaches for diagnosis and treatment.

In many situations, doctors and patients do not have a statistical basis for assessing these factors. Many issues have never been studied. For example, we do not know whether the survival rate of heart attack patients increases significantly if they are seen once a month by a cardiologist rather than once every six months. We do not know the probability that an MRI exam for someone with lower back pain will lead to a treatment that would not otherwise have been ordered.

As we saw in Chapter 1 on premium medicine, spending on apparently similar patient populations varies considerably across regions of the country. According to John Wennberg, Medicare spends vastly different amounts on patients during the last six months of life, depending on where the patients live:

- For individual hospitals, the average number of days that a patient spends in intensive care in the last six months of life ranges from a low of 1.6 to a high of 9.5.
- The proportion of patients seeing 10 or more physicians in the last six months of life ranges from a low of 17 percent to a high of 58 percent.

Overall, Wennberg writes, "Per enrollee Medicare spending varies almost threefold among hospital referral regions and academic medical centers."[9] In the absence of data to guide decisions, this is not surprising. Doctors can use different rules of thumb if there is no body of evidence that favors one approach over another.

Specifying a medical protocol for the purpose of statistical analysis can be tricky. In theory, one wants a database entry that states the condition the patient presented, the procedure that the doctor ordered, and the outcome. In practice, the condition itself may be viewed differently by different doctors. The patient may or may not follow the procedure. The assessment of the outcome may be subjective. These difficulties may help to explain the fact that consumers cannot find ratings for physicians that are as accessible and usable as ratings for cars or personal computers.

In Chapter 8, "Policy Ideas," I will address the need to obtain statistical information that relates health care outcomes to health care practices. Only with such information can premium medicine be evaluated and practiced rationally.

4. No Perfect Health Care System

Here is a key point to consider:

- Any health care system must reflect a compromise of preferences. We cannot have health care that is both accessible and affordable while insulating consumers from the cost.

Broadly speaking, there are two areas of concern with regard to health care finance. First, is the financing system efficient, in the economic sense that the correct share of resources is devoted to health care and those resources are used cost-effectively? Second, is the distributional outcome acceptable, or are there severe inequities in access to health care resources?

In principle, the question of efficiency can be answered objectively using economic concepts. The question of distribution is more subjective, since there is no standard definition of what constitutes distributional equity in health care.

In many industrialized countries, less than 20 percent of health care expenditures are paid for directly by consumers. In the United States, for example, about 86 percent of health care spending is paid for by someone other than the patient, usually government or private insurance.[1] The challenge, faced by all countries' health care systems, is that third-party payments take away important incentives for efficiency. When someone else is paying, the consumer does not need to focus on the cost of health care treatment.

In the United States, our concerns about distributional inequities are focused on the poor and the uninsured. It is important not to confuse the two. In general, poor people are eligible for government health programs, such as Medicaid. Many of the uninsured are people who are not eligible for Medicaid, either because their incomes are too high or because they lack citizenship status. Many of the uninsured believe that the cost of health insurance is high relative to the probability that they will need it. Young people in good health have good reason to feel this way, although many believe that forgoing insurance in the hope of remaining healthy is an unwise choice.

In addition to the goals of efficiency and equity, there are certain characteristics of the health care system in America that are culturally embedded. Americans deeply resent limitations on availability of health care services, which is why managed care provokes controversy and proposals to ration health care are not popular. Americans also have become accustomed to not having to pay for health care services out of pocket. Instead, we have come to expect that most of our health care spending will be paid for by either private insurance or government programs.

Of course, if the average American consumes $5,000 in health care services per year, then the average American also pays for $5,000 in health care services per year. If we only pay $750 per year out of pocket, then we pay the rest through insurance premiums and taxes.

Given the economic goals of efficiency and equitable distribution, along with the cultural expectations that have developed in the United States, there is no perfect way to finance health care. There are fundamental tradeoffs with which every system must contend. To see this, let me propose a straw man: a set of three principles that "must" be satisfied by a perfect health care system.

- *Unfettered Access.* Consumers must be completely free to select any treatment that the health care provider and patient agree would be beneficial.
- *Insulation.* Consumers must be protected from the financial and emotional burden of paying for health care procedures. They should have the security of knowing that health care will be provided by private insurance and/or government.
- *Affordability.* The health care system must not absorb an inordinate amount of resources. Health care spending should not crowd out more valuable public- or private-sector needs.

It should be readily apparent that these three principles are not mutually compatible. If consumers are to have unfettered access to treatment but be insulated from cost, then consumer demand would be limited only by the nonmonetary costs (such as the inconvenience of going to the doctor) of obtaining health care services. Therefore, the system would not be affordable.

In our current system, all three principles appear to be compromised. Both private and government insurance programs place restrictions on treatments, so that there is not unfettered access. Many consumers are uninsured, so they are not insulated. The most dramatic problem, at least relative to other countries, concerns affordability. Health care spending as a proportion of GDP stands at 15 percent in the United States, and it is growing rapidly.

No feasible health care system can fully satisfy the three principles. One or more of the principles must be compromised. To put it bluntly, a health care finance system must inevitably be imperfect. We have an imperfect system now. Any alternative will be imperfect. One way to look at alternative health care finance systems is to imagine what would happen if one were willing to sacrifice one of the three principles. By completely sacrificing one of the principles, an alternative health care finance system can be devised.

Restricting Access

Suppose that we were willing to place no weight on the principle of unfettered access. In that case, we could create a system in which consumers are insulated from paying for health care procedures while keeping the system affordable. The solution would be to have government set a budget that limits the supply of health care services. Bureaucrats would set health care priorities. Inevitably, some consumers would be denied treatments that they seek. To obtain unauthorized treatments, consumers would have to go outside the system, presumably paying for treatments themselves.

Many Americans would resist health care rationing, and properly so. We should not automatically assume that the American approach that seeks immediate and definitive treatment is wrong. Although premium medicine raises the cost of health care, in many cases it is cost-effective. However, if the goal is to insulate consumers from cost while keeping health care affordable in the aggregate, then premium medicine will have to be curtailed. Americans are not very comfortable with the idea of health care decisions being made for them by third parties. In the 1990s, when managed care was introduced as a way to restrain the growth of health care spending, there was widespread backlash.

Even Americans who accept the idea of health care rationing in principle may be reluctant to accept it in practice. We may never have a true single-payer health care system in which all health care is paid for by the government. Instead, some consumers may seek treatment that goes beyond what the government will provide. This might lead to a health care system that looks somewhat like our primary education system. Parents who are particularly wealthy or demanding choose private schools over public schools. Similarly, we can expect that many consumers and doctors will be reluctant to accept restrictions on access that are imposed under a government-run health care financing system. We would have a two-tier system, in which some people use government-funded health care and others use private health care.

In summary, trying to make health care more affordable by restricting access through bureaucratic rationing faces several challenges. First, it may be that it is the countries that ration health care that have it wrong. Perhaps our heavy utilization of diagnostic procedures and treatments, expensive as these may be, is cost-effective—or at least less costly than denying treatment to many who want it. Second, many Americans believe that people should be free to obtain whatever health care they think they need, and we resent bureaucratic intrusion. Finally, even those Americans who believe in health care rationing in principle may take a different view when it involves their own health or that of their loved ones.

Paying Up

Another approach to health care would be to sacrifice the principle of affordability. In some ways, David Cutler makes this proposal in his book, *Your Money or Your Life*.[2] Cutler argues that health care spending produces increases in what he calls "quality-adjusted life-years." In fact, he would argue that we spend too *little* on health care, at least for the poor and the uninsured. We could improve our health care system by spending more on these underserved populations.

To be fair, Cutler also proposes reforms aimed at reducing waste and excess in health care spending. His primary suggestion is to shift some of the compensation of health care providers away from fee-for-service reimbursement and toward bonuses based on measures of health care quality. Still, Cutler makes no claim that these reforms would mitigate the fiscal impact of his proposals to expand health care coverage. Instead, he states quite explicitly that we should be prepared to dedicate more tax revenue to health care.

There are several problems with sacrificing the principle of affordability. First, for the United States, sacrificing affordability would mean moving even farther away than we are now from the expenditure patterns of other industrialized nations. While almost no other advanced country spends more than 10 percent of its GDP on health care, the United States spends 15 percent. It would be comforting to see more evidence of the cost-effectiveness of our health care before we commit to increasing this share still further.

Second, many would argue that we have already gone too far in this direction, and that further sacrificing affordability would worsen our current problems. Our employer-provided private health insurance system is already fraying. Largely because of health care costs, firms' cost of compensation is rising faster than inflation, even though what workers take home in wages is not. In order to try to limit health care costs, firms are hiring fewer full-time workers. The proportion of the labor force covered by health insurance is declining, as people are increasingly employed as independent consultants, temporary workers, and other positions not under a corporate umbrella.

Government is finding it increasingly difficult to fund its major health care programs: Medicare and Medicaid. Medicare spending exceeds its dedicated tax collections, which means that Medicare must be funded in part out of general revenues. This funding gap threatens to grow rapidly over the next several decades. Medicaid is taking an ever-rising share of state and federal budgets.[3]

Cutler has some persuasive arguments for the view that heroic, expensive medical treatments often pay off. However, the combination of unfettered access and insulation provides little incentive for cost-benefit analysis. The more funds that are made available from third parties, such as government, the more gray area tests and procedures will be performed for which the expected benefits are less than the costs.

Removing Insulation

A final possibility would be to sacrifice the principle of insulation. The idea would be to encourage more people to pay for more of their health care out of pocket. Healthy middle-class families would

49

control their own health care dollars and be responsible for more of their own health care costs. Only the very poor and the very sick would have health care paid for by taxpayers. Without insulation, people would be expected to save for the health care that they are likely to need as they age. Most seniors would neither receive Medicare nor have their nursing home care paid for by Medicaid. Instead, they would use a combination of savings and private insurance to cover those needs.

Private insurance would more closely resemble catastrophic coverage. Most people would not make any health insurance claims in a typical year. Rather, they would only file claims when they require costly medical care. The government would provide cash or vouchers to the poor to enable them to obtain health care. However, government would not provide any assistance, either directly or through subsidies, to people who have the means to pay for health care themselves.

Removing the insulation that consumers have from health care costs would change the way that health care decisions are made. Doctors and patients would have to agree on the costs and benefits of diagnostic procedures, rather than carrying them out as if there were no cost. Under such circumstances, it might become acceptable once again for an internist to say "wait and see" before referring a patient to a specialist or ordering an MRI. With less health care paid for by third parties, it would be possible to reconcile the principle of affordability with the principle of unfettered access. Doctors and patients would choose the diagnostic procedures and treatments that they believe are cost-effective.

For an economist, it makes sense to sacrifice the principle of insulation to promote unfettered access and affordability. The principle of access unfettered by bureaucratic intrusion is consistent with consumer choice, free trade, and other concepts that economists hold dear. The principle of affordability also has an obvious economic appeal. However, the principle of insulation has little or no economic justification. In fact, I think that the task for economists, and for Chapter 5 of this book, is to explain the high cost and dubious benefits of catering to the principle of insulation.

5. Insulation vs. Insurance

Here are seven key points to consider:

- The rise of premium medicine makes the issue of insulation more significant than ever.
- True insurance would cover only large, unpredictable expenses, and would provide long-term catastrophic coverage. Health care plans that cover small and predictable expenses provide prepaid routine care in addition to insurance.
- Insulation provides an incentive to overconsume health care services in the gray area, where the service is not absolutely necessary and may not be cost-effective.
- What we call "health insurance" is probably misunderstood by consumers. For example, workers may not realize that their take-home pay is reduced as employers pay for health insurance.
- The high likelihood that the elderly will incur large medical expenses makes it more of a predictable event and less of an insurable one.
- Doctors are understandably comfortable with an insurance system that reimburses them for procedures. However, this is probably not the best system of physician compensation.
- Changing from our current system to one of real health insurance would be difficult. Congress would need to realign incentives and remove some regulatory barriers.

Imagine one had something called "eating insurance." Under such a plan, whether the premiums are paid by the government, the employer, or the individual, a person would not have to pay for food at any restaurant. One could order whatever he or she wants, and eating insurance would pay. This form of "insurance" is most beneficial to restaurant owners. They can offer premium food, knowing that the consumer is insulated from the cost.

What we think of as health insurance is similar. It does not really serve the economic purpose of insurance. Instead, it acts as a cost insulation system. There are many reasons why health "insurance" evolved this way in the United States.

The Blue Cross and Blue Shield programs, which inaugurated health insurance in the United States, were in fact created mostly for the benefit of health care providers.[1] Hospitals and doctors were able to obtain reliable payment from these prepaid health plans. Up until 1950, the consumer need for health care insurance was minimal. Health care could do much less, and so it cost much less. Open-heart surgery, like many other expensive procedures, had not yet been developed.

Today, the availability of expensive, premium medicine means there is more that medicine can do for us. It also means there are more potential costs to insure against. However, these genuine needs are not met by what emerged as health insurance in the 1950s. Rather than build on the legacy of cost insulation, we ought to start from scratch and reinvent health insurance.

Insulation and the Gray Area

In the United States, consumers tend to be heavily insulated from having to pay health expenses out of pocket. In 2002, Americans paid for only 14 percent of their health care expenses directly, a lower percentage than Japanese (16.5 percent) or Canadians (15.2 percent). The remaining 86 percent of U.S. health care spending was covered by third parties (e.g., government and private insurance).

Among major industrial countries, only Germany (with 10.4 percent of expenses paid for out of pocket) and France (with 9.8 percent) went further than the United States in insulating consumers from health care payments. Insulation of consumers from health care costs is a feature of health systems around the world.[2]

Insulation affects the consumption of health care services that fall in the gray area. As described in Chapter 2, a health care procedure falls in the gray area if it has a positive benefit that nonetheless may be less than the cost of the procedure. When a procedure falls in the gray area, and a consumer is insulated from the cost of that procedure, the consumer will elect to undergo the procedure. If the consumer is not insulated from the cost, then the consumer may elect otherwise. For example, a precautionary MRI might be undertaken if insurance will pay for it, but the consumer might forgo the MRI if it has to be paid for out of pocket.

Third-party payers, meaning insurance companies and government health spending agencies, do not have a clear mandate to police the gray area. On the one hand, third-party payers are entitled to crack down on fraudulent billing practices and totally unnecessary procedures—what I refer to as the "black region" of health care. On the other hand, declining to pay for a procedure in the gray area is much more problematic. Refusing to cover treatment that offers small, positive benefits can cause friction with consumers and could expose the payer to unfavorable publicity and/or a legal challenge. Outside of the United States, it is more common for governments to try to control gray-area medical procedures.

The rise of premium medicine makes the issue of insulation more significant than ever. With advanced technology and skilled specialists abundantly available, there are more (and more expensive) gray-area services. Consumer insulation means that there is no mechanism in place to limit the demand for health care services to those that are cost-effective. As noted in Chapter 5, there is no way to reconcile insulation, affordability, and availability. Either supply has to be restrained by a national health care budget, demand has to be restrained by giving consumers less insulation from costs, or the nation's health care spending will grow unchecked.

What this chapter will show is that the goal of health insurance, which is protecting consumers from the risk of financially crippling health care expenses, might be achieved with much less insulation of consumers from gray-area health care costs. That is, market forces can be used to contain the growth in health care spending without denying people access to necessary care.

Insurance and Risk Aversion

From an economic perspective, risk aversion is a valid reason for people to pool their resources on health care. In any group of, say, ten thousand people, chosen at random, perhaps only about one hundred will develop unusually expensive ailments before age 65. A risk-averse individual would be willing to join an insurance pool, paying a small premium to be covered for a really large loss.

Risk aversion justifies insurance against expenses that are large and infrequent. In cases such as fire hazard, only a few policyholders make claims. If health insurance worked the same way, then benefits would rarely be paid out. Large but *predictable* expenses, such as the cost of obstetrics for a normal baby, are not risks that can be spread, so they are not insurable. *Unpredictable* expenses, such as the cost of caring for a high-risk infant, are more properly considered an insurable risk. Unpredictable but small expenses, such as the cost of diagnosis and treatment for strep throat, are inappropriate for insurance. Because the cost is low, even a risk-averse consumer would not pay an insurance premium to protect against such expenses.

Our current system of health insurance bears very little resemblance to a system that would be designed to satisfy risk aversion. Many small and predictable expenses are paid for by both private and government health care plans. At the same time, some of the biggest medical risks that people face are not covered. When a health plan administrator brags about the insurance at his or her company or government agency, the examples that illustrate the quality of the plan are often instances in which small expenses are covered: payments for eyeglasses or routine dental exams, for example. Many people seem to equate the concept of "good health insurance" to the breadth of minor expenses that are covered by the plan.

People often find, however, that major illnesses can threaten them with financial ruin. Under the current system of employer-provided health insurance, losing one's job may mean that a person is unable to obtain insurance for a "preexisting condition." Few people in their 40s and 50s have long-term care insurance, even though a major disability causes more economic hardship and is more of a surprise at that age than when someone is in their 70s or 80s. Rational risk aversion would lead to a very different form of health insurance than what we observe today. Risk aversion would lead to a health insurance policy that, like fire insurance, pays claims relatively infrequently but protects the consumer against severe catastrophe.

Health insurance with a high deductible, called catastrophic coverage, is one logical approach for protecting consumers from serious risk. Economists have also considered more sophisticated forms of insurance, such as insurance against being diagnosed with an expensive disease, insurance against discovering that one's genetic makeup is likely to lead to costly illness, or insurance that protects against an increase in the cost of renewing one's insurance.[3]

Insulation and the Law of Demand

The law of demand states that when the price of a good or service falls, people consume more of it. The law of demand predicts that if people are insulated from the cost of health care services, because insurance will pay for them, then people will consume more of them. Does the law of demand apply to health care? Some people say that it does, some people say that it does not, and some people argue both ways without recognizing the contradiction.[4]

One might doubt that the law of demand applies to health care. It may seem logical that when you need health care, you obtain it regardless of cost. When you do not need health care, you do not waste time getting it, even if it is free.

In practice, however, this either-or distinction breaks down. With individual health care decisions, it is often *not* the case that you either need it or you don't. In many instances, there is no clear line between what is necessary and what is frivolous. As noted in Chapter 3, choices about diagnostic and treatment protocols can be quite complex. Six months after heart surgery, how often should you be seeing a cardiologist? Perhaps it is only necessary to have a follow-up once a year. However, if it costs nothing, then you might prefer to have a follow-up once a month. Sometimes a doctor thinks that an MRI is unlikely to uncover anything, but it might be a sensible precaution. The deciding factor can be whether the MRI is covered by insurance or whether the patient will have to pay out of pocket.

Whether the law of demand applies to health care was tested in a famous experiment by RAND. It assigned consumers to different insurance policies, and then it compared the health spending decisions of those who were more insulated from costs with the decisions of those who were required to pay a share of their health care costs. The conclusion was that "cost sharing reduced care but had little effect on health."[5]

It can be argued that the law of demand is a bad thing in health care. The concern is that consumers will forgo important health procedures, especially preventive care, unless they are insulated from its cost.

A realistic perspective is that the law of demand does operate in health care. People spend less on health care when their own money is involved. One might hope that they are unlikely to reduce spending on necessary acute care, and instead will reduce spending on optional services. When a consumer decides that the expected benefits of a health care service are below its cost, then it is rational for the consumer to forgo that service. However, that does not mean that the expected benefits of the forgone service are zero. Forgone health care services represent a real reduction in health care. What standard economic analysis suggests, however, is that the resources are better used somewhere else.

Nonetheless, there is evidence to suggest that charging patients will cause some people to forgo necessary care.[6] To me, this suggests trying to make health care accessible at a low cost to the poor. However, I have no policy prescription for the circumstance in which people are sufficiently affluent to afford treatment but nonetheless will forgo cost-effective health care if they have to pay for it.

Why Doctors Prefer Insulation

Doctors prefer to work in an environment in which they do not have to charge patients for services. They would rather make their best judgments about what the patient needs and be reimbursed for their services by a third party. Of course, suppliers in other industries would like to operate in a similar context. A restaurant owner would prefer to serve diners who are on an expense account. The owner can recommend the best food and wine, without having to take cost into consideration.

From a doctor's perspective, the ideal form of health insurance would provide reliable payment without the doctor being second-guessed by patients or insurance companies concerning the value of a treatment plan relative to its cost. For this reason, doctors may prefer insulation to real health insurance.

True Health Insurance

From an economic perspective, real health insurance would differ from what we call health insurance today, in the following ways:

- Real health insurance would cover major expenses, not minor ones.
- Real health insurance would be there when it is most needed— for major, long-term illnesses.
- Real health insurance would be in force for long periods of time. It would reduce or eliminate "renewal risk"—the risk that a consumer will not be able to afford to renew his or her

health insurance policy.[7] It would also give insurance providers a stake in the long-term health of the consumer, leading insurance companies to encourage consumers to obtain appropriate checkups, exercise, and so forth.

True health insurance would be something like long-term catastrophic health insurance. That is, there would be a high deductible, and both the deductible and the insurance coverage could span several years.

There are many ways to address the problem of renewal risk. For example, John Cochrane[8] has suggested that a health insurance contract could combine two forms of insurance: insurance that pays for large expenses while the policy is in effect, and insurance that pays for an increase in the individual's expected future health care expenses after the policy lapses. Thus, if I develop a long-term illness that is going to drive up my future health care premiums, my current policy would pay not just for my near-term health costs but also for the long-term increase in premiums, either by not increasing my premiums or by offering me a severance payment that would cover my higher premiums with another insurer. While Cochrane's analysis shows that an "optimal" contract can be written to address renewal risk, I believe that in practice the problem can be addressed with an approach that does not require payments based on forecasts of future insurance needs.

For example, suppose that my health care expenses follow the pattern in Table 5-1. Each year I might obtain a five-year health insurance policy with a deductible of $30,000. The premiums I pay in the first year provide me with a five-year umbrella of coverage. However, each year, I purchase another five-year umbrella, so that I am covered by an overlapping set of five-year umbrellas.

The first year that I meet the five-year deductible is 2010. The insurance policy that I paid for in 2006 would be responsible for reimbursing me the $2,000 difference between my five-year expenses in 2010 of $32,000 and the five-year deductible of $30,000. The insurance policy that I paid for in 2007 (which might be from the same company or a different company) would be responsible for the $1,000 difference between my five-year expenses in 2011 of $31,000 and the $30,000 deductible. If my five-year expenses remain more than $30,000 in 2012, then my 2008 insurance policy would make up the difference.[9]

Table 5-1
MULTIYEAR HEALTH INSURANCE POLICIES

Year	Expenses	Five-Year Expenses
2005	$2,000	—
2006	$5,000	—
2007	$5,000	—
2008	$4,000	—
2009	$10,000	$26,000
2010	$8,000	$32,000
2011	$4,000	$31,000

Most people under age 65 could obtain these sorts of long-term catastrophic health insurance policies at reasonable rates. The high deductible means that premiums could be low and consumers would have more money to save for out-of-pocket expenses. Because no one is in a position to be highly confident that they will avoid catastrophic illness for five years, the potential problem of information asymmetry—where patients know more about their future health expenditures than insurers do—ought to be mitigated.

Even though each insurance policy would cover five years of expenses, the consumer would have a sequence of policies in force at any given time. The consumer obtains a five-year policy in 2005, another five-year policy in 2006, and so on. That means that if the consumer incurs a long-term illness starting in 2009, the fourth year of the first policy, the consumer will not be bereft of insurance in 2011. In 2011, the policies obtained in 2006, 2007, and 2008 will still be in force. Thus, even long-term illnesses would be protected against the risk of not being able to renew one's health insurance.

People with long-term, expensive illnesses, such as diabetes, would still have difficulty finding affordable health insurance under the scheme just proposed. There might be an alternative scheme that provides better protection. Alternatively, there could be a separate type of insurance that covers the event of being diagnosed with long-term, expensive illnesses. Nonetheless, it could turn out, particularly during a transition period from our current insulation-focused system to a system of true health insurance, that people with long-term illnesses may require government vouchers to enable them to purchase health insurance.

Figure 5-1
PERSONAL HEALTH SPENDING PER CAPITA BY AGE, 2002

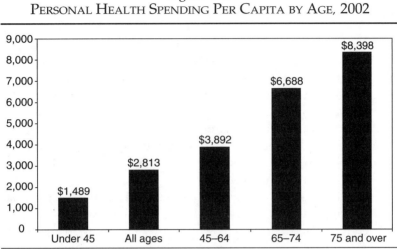

SOURCE: 2002 Medical Expenditure Panel Survey data.

Insurance, Insulation, and Age

Another way Americans have become accustomed to insulation from health care costs is through Medicare. As with employer-provided health insurance, Medicare provides coverage that goes well beyond the rationale for risk mitigation.

As people age, they require more health care. In the 2002 Medical Expenditure Panel Survey (MEPS), overall personal health spending per capita was $2,813. For people under age 45, the average was $1,489. For people age 45–64, the average was $3,892. For people age 65–74, the average was $6,688. For people age 75 and over, the average was $8,398.[10] Thus, we see clearly the pattern of spending increasing by age. To the extent that everyone spends more on health care as they get older, this is not an insurable risk. It is simply an expense for which one must plan (see Figure 5-1).

In a sense, the elderly incur two types of health costs, which we might call regular care and late-stage care. Regular care occurs as long as people remain free of debilitating illness. Late-stage care deals with terminal cancer, Alzheimer's, and other diseases that require full-time assistance, often in a nursing home. Unfortunately, the odds of avoiding high late-stage health costs are not very good.

As we live longer, the diseases that kill us tend to be more debilitating. Joanne Lynn and David Adamson write that "Americans will usually spend two or more of their final years disabled enough to need someone else to help with routine activities of daily living."[11]

Alastair Gray summarizes research suggesting that health care costs are determined more by proximity to death than by age.[12] This is consistent with the view that the uncertainty regarding health care costs among those over age 65 is more a matter of "when" than "if." David Cutler and Richard Zeckhauser note that "Nearly 20 percent of people over age 85 are in a nursing home, compared to about 1 percent of the population aged 65 to 74."[13] To the extent that this is so, insurance becomes quite difficult.

One person might be struck by a debilitating illness at age 70. Another might be struck at age 90. In any given year, the variation in spending could be high. However, after age 65, the variation in *lifetime* health care spending may not be sufficiently high to create a real insurance pool.

Geoffrey F. Joyce and colleagues have estimated that remaining lifetime health expenditures for those who reach age 65 average about $105,000.[14] David Cutler comments on their paper as follows:

> Why so much? There are two important reasons. First, virtually everyone winds up with some chronic disease ultimately, and chronic disease is very costly. Even healthy people at age sixty-five develop arthritis, suffer broken bones, or have heart attacks. About half of people age eighty-five and older, for example, have a limitation in either activities of daily living (ADLs) or instrumental activities of daily living (IADLs). People with one or two ADL limitations spend twice what the nondisabled do annually. Second, death is very expensive—more accurately, people get very sick before they die, and being very sick is quite costly. Joyce and colleagues show that about one-quarter of lifetime medical costs for the elderly occur in the last year of life.[15]

If high expenditures on health care before death are nearly inevitable, then real insurance is not possible. How should these expenditures be paid for? Current policy is that health care for the elderly should be paid for by government, through taxes on working people. The reasoning is approximately as follows:

- The elderly need health "insurance."
- The elderly are not working, so they cannot afford insurance.
- Therefore, the government needs to step in and provide health insurance to the elderly.

What this leads to is not really health insurance for the elderly. Instead, the elderly are merely insulated from health care costs. As inevitable as their high expenditures might be, the elderly do not have to save for these costs, because of a social contract that says that the health care of the elderly will be provided by taxes on those who are working.

Remaining Lifetime Catastrophic Insurance

For people over age 65, the best form of health insurance might be Remaining Lifetime Catastrophic Insurance (RLCI). One would pay annual premiums for a policy with a very large deductible, perhaps $50,000 or $100,000. The deductible would be met by cumulative expenses incurred after age 65.

RLCI might work as follows. An individual between age 30 and age 65 would save $1,600 a year. At an inflation- and tax-adjusted interest rate of 3 percent per year, this would leave just over $100,000 at age 65. With an earlier start date for savings, the annual amount needed to reach a goal of $100,000 would be lower. Other assets, including home equity, could be used to amass this amount. An individual retains $75,000 to pay for out-of-pocket expenses and plans to spend $25,000 on premiums for RLCI with a lifetime deductible of $75,000. After having spent the $75,000 on health care expenses, the individual's insurance policy takes over and pays all further expenses.

One challenge with offering RLCI is that changes in medical technology could have major effects. If a company sells RLCI to a cohort that is age 65 today, and 10 years from now a really expensive medical procedure becomes available that is demanded by many in the cohort who have survived to that point, the insurance company would face costs that are much higher than expected. In fact, David Cutler has argued that this technology risk, because it is nondiversifiable, is one reason that we do not observe long-term contracts in health insurance.[16]

In theory, the government could offer RLCI by changing Medicare to a catastrophic insurance program. However, catastrophic insurance can be less attractive to politicians than broad-based subsidies.

Programs that offer frequent subsidies to large constituencies (e.g., prescription drug subsidies for seniors) are more popular than programs that provide more sporadic subsidies to smaller constituencies (e.g., subsidies for catastrophic health expenses, which only a portion of seniors will incur in any given year).

Insurance Reform

The examples of five-year cumulative health insurance and remaining lifetime catastrophic insurance show that it is possible for true health insurance to be workable. That is, we could have health insurance that protects people against the cost of expensive illness without insulating them against less costly medical bills.

Unfortunately, it would be a real challenge to get from here to there. The legacy of insulation is embedded in government health care programs, labor contracts, government policies that encourage employer-provided health insurance, and state insurance regulations that mandate coverage of specific services. In Chapter 8, I offer a few suggestions that might allow true health insurance to emerge instead.

6. Matching Funding Systems to Needs

Here are four key points to consider:

- Using the Medical Expenditure Panel Survey (MEPS), we can divide the population into the very poor, the very sick, and neither.
- If government financing of health care were focused on the very poor, government health care spending would be much lower than is the case today.
- Private health insurance could pay the cost of insuring the very sick (meaning those with catastrophic expenses) while accounting for less spending overall than it does today.
- About half of medical expenses could be paid out of pocket by people who are neither very poor nor very sick.

The idea of matching the health care funding system to needs is very simple. The very poor and the very sick need help paying for health care. The rest of us do not. The very poor need help paying medical bills. People with expensive, permanent illnesses, such as diabetes, also fall in this category. Support for the poor and the permanently ill could come from private charity, but here I will assume that it comes from government. I term as "very sick" people who run into unusually large medical bills in a given year, but who are not permanently ill. Catastrophic health insurance is the ideal solution for dealing with the expenses that arise when someone becomes very sick.

For people who are not poor and whose medical expenses are not unusually large, paying for medical care out of pocket is reasonable. Shifting responsibility to others only introduces administrative costs and economic distortions.

To summarize, I propose the following approach for matching funding systems to needs (see Table 6-1).

To analyze the allocation of the health care funding system to needs, I will use the Medical Expenditure Panel Survey for 2002.

Table 6-1
PROPOSED SOURCES OF HEALTH CARE FUNDING FOR
DIFFERENT POPULATIONS

Category of Needs	Proposed Source for Health Care Funding
The very poor and the permanently ill	Government
The very sick	Private health insurance
Neither very poor nor very sick	Out-of-pocket payments

MEPS uses a survey of roughly 35,000 Americans to extrapolate medical expenditures for the entire noninstitutional population. According to MEPS, for the population as a whole, the median level of health care spending per capita was $663, and the mean was $2,813. (Note that the mean is well above the median. This indicates that the distribution is skewed, which suggests a potential for insurance.) Total spending was $811 billion.

Ideally, we would like to use lifetime income and lifetime health expenditures to assess poverty and sickness. However, the MEPS panel of respondents changes each year, so that it is not possible to use a multiyear definition of "very poor" or to distinguish the permanently ill from the very sick. I will instead use annual income and annual health expenditures. The definition of "very poor" will be individuals with family incomes at or below the poverty line in 2002. In the MEPS, this would be extrapolated to 35.6 million people. This is not the best definition of "very poor" for a variety of reasons, primarily because incomes fluctuate from year to year. It also does not include assets. A long-term measure of poverty would be more accurate, but then the MEPS was not constructed with that in mind.

For the very poor, median health care spending in 2002 was $372 and the mean was $2,985. Note that the mean is above the national average, although the median is not. Total health care spending among the poor was $106 billion. The MEPS shows that of that $106 billion, the poor paid $14 billion out of pocket and had another $14 billion paid by private health insurance. Both figures are surprisingly high, particularly the out-of-pocket payments.

The fact that the median level of health care spending by the poor is below the national median may indicate that the poor spend too little on preventive care. Suppose that per capita health care spending on the poor rose by $200, which would bring the median spending for the poor more in line with the national median. That would increase health care spending on the poor by $7 billion to $113 billion. One could argue that matching the funding system to needs would require government to spend this much on the poor.

The definition of "very sick" changes with age. For individuals under age 65, median health care spending in 2002 was $506, and the mean was $2,137. For individuals age 65 and over, the median was $3,337 and the mean was $7,509. The fact that the ratio of the median to the mean is higher for the elderly (0.44) than for the nonelderly (.024) suggests that high health care costs are less of an insurable event for the old than for the young.[1]

In Chapter 5, I proposed long-term catastrophic insurance, with a deductible of $30,000 for the nonelderly and a deductible of $75,000 for the elderly. Because the MEPS data only cover one year, in this chapter I need to adapt the idea to one year of spending. Here, I use an annual deductible of $5,000 for the nonelderly and $20,000 for the elderly.

Suppose that government were to pay for all health care spending for the poor and that everyone under age 65 obtained a catastrophic health insurance policy with a $5,000 deductible, and everyone age 65 or older obtained a policy with a deductible of $20,000. Then, using the MEPS data, there is $811 billion of total spending. (As noted earlier, this total is less than the amount in the National Health Accounts, with the largest portion of the discrepancy due to the fact that MEPS omits the expenditures of many who are in nursing homes.) Table 6-2 shows the proposed division of expenditures.

Table 6-3 compares the actual sources of expenditure with the proposal in Table 6-2, by category. Format is actual/proposed.[2]

Figure 6-1 visually depicts how the sources of health care funding would change for each category of patient.

The result of aligning funding sources to needs would be as follows: reduce the government share of health care spending on the noninstitutional population from 40 percent to 13 percent; reduce the share of health care spending on the noninstitutional population accounted for by private health insurance from 41 percent to 31 percent; increase the share of health care spending paid for out of pocket from 19 percent to 56 percent.

Table 6-2
PROPOSED DISTRIBUTION OF HEALTH CARE SPENDING FOR
DIFFERENT POPULATIONS BY SOURCE, 2002

	Very Poor	Not Very Poor		Not Very Poor		Total
		65+	65+	<65	<65	
		Very Sick	Not Very Sick	Very Sick	Not Very Sick	
Population (millions)	35.6	3.9	28.5	21.1	t199.2	288.3
Sources of Spending ($billions)						
Government	$106*	$0	$0	$0	$0	$106
Private insurance	$0	$71	$0	$183	$0	$254
Out of pocket	$0	$59	$109	$105	$178	$451
Total	$106	$130	$109	$288	$178	$811

SOURCE: Medical Expenditure Panel Survey, 2002, and author's calculations.
*As noted previously, perhaps this figure ought to be $113 billion, if we assume the poor are not receiving enough health care.

Aligning funding sources to needs in this way would have a number of advantages:

- The financial strain on government would be greatly reduced.
- The system of employer-financed health insurance, which is becoming harder to sustain, would be relieved.
- A larger share of medical care would be paid for out of pocket, which would increase the incentive for consumers to evaluate the cost-effectiveness of care.
- Savings would increase, because people would be saving for health care and health insurance in their old age, rather than counting on Medicare.
- The poor would pay less out of pocket than they do today. Those who believe that the poor underconsume health care would argue that this will lead to better decisions on the part of the poor. It is possible, however, that this would lead the

Table 6-3
DISTRIBUTION OF HEALTH CARE SPENDING FOR DIFFERENT POPULATIONS, BY SOURCE, ACTUAL VERSUS PROPOSED, 2002

Age category	Very Poor	Not Very Poor 65+		Not Very Poor <65		Total	%
		Very Sick	Not Very Sick	Very Sick	Not Very Sick		
Population (millions)	35.6	3.9	28.5	21.1	199.2	288.3	100
Sources of Spending: Actual/Proposed ($ billions)							
Government	$78/$106	$103/$0	$54/$0	$71/$0	$19/$0	$325/$106	40/13
Private insurance	$14/$0	$18/$71	$22/$0	$178/$183	$99/$0	$331/$254	41/31
Out-of-pocket	$14/$0	$9/$59	$33/$109	$39/$105	$60/$178	$155/$451	19/56
Total	$106	$130	$109	$288	$178	$811	100

SOURCE: Medical Expenditure Panel Survey, 2002, and author's calculations

Figure 6-1
SOURCES OF NONINSTITUTIONAL HEALTH SPENDING,
CURRENT VS. PROPOSED

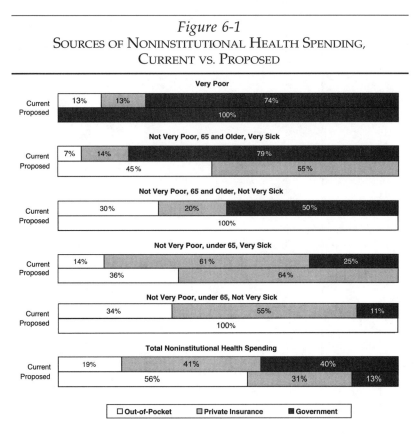

poor to overconsume health care in the gray area. There is also the important issue of designing assistance to the poor in a way that does not induce dependence on government and discourage recipients from helping themselves.

One would hope that reducing third-party payments would lead to lower spending. However, this analysis takes the current level of spending as given. Some health care plans, such as that proposed during the first term of the Clinton administration, presume unspecified savings in health care spending. Certainly, there is nothing wrong with reducing waste in health care. However, I believe that it is more prudent to propose a health care financing system that assumes the same level of spending undertaken currently.

Practical Policy Approaches

Compared with our current health care finance system, a system that matches funding to needs would offer less comprehensive health insurance and more catastrophic coverage. It would also replace Medicare with personal savings, means-tested government support, and perhaps government-provided Remaining Lifetime Catastrophic Insurance.

The government could take a number of steps to encourage a shift from comprehensive health insurance to catastrophic coverage. The catastrophic insurance I have in mind is a five-year policy with a cumulative deductible. Over the five-year term of the policy, the consumer might be responsible for 100 percent of cumulative expenses below $15,000, 50 percent of expenses between $15,000 and $30,000, and none of the expenses beyond that. The insurance company would pick up the remainder. Call this the Model Policy.

As another alternative, health insurance companies could offer policies that work like some forms of automobile insurance: if you develop an ailment, a claims adjuster could come out, do a "damage assessment," and send you a check. Policies that work like this currently are being marketed as "critical care" insurance.[3]

In order to eliminate Medicare, I would recommend an approach that phases out Medicare through graduated increases in the age of eligibility. People born in 1950 (meaning that they are 55 in 2005) might have their eligibility left unchanged. People born in 1980 would not be eligible for Medicare at all. For people born between 1950 and 1980, the age of eligibility would increase by six months for each year they were born after 1950. Thus, someone born in 1970 would be eligible for Medicare at an age 10 years older (age 75) than someone born in 1950 (age 65).

To replace Medicare, government policy should encourage more saving. Savings accounts to pay for health care after age 65 should be tax-favored, and perhaps mandatory. For example, as young workers are phased out of Medicare, their Medicare payroll taxes might instead be directed toward health savings accounts. Government could monitor the market for Remaining Lifetime Catastrophic Insurance. To the extent that portions of the elderly population are unable to obtain such coverage, government could provide it.

Summary

The goals of providing health care to the poor and providing economic security to those with high medical expenses can be achieved with much less government spending on health care than is done today. Better alignment of health care financing to needs would

- Reduce the burden of health care on state and federal budgets in which the rapid growth of Medicaid and Medicare has outstripped tax collections and will otherwise require large tax increases.
- Increase the proportion of spending for which consumers pay directly, rather than collectively through insurance and taxes, thereby improving the incentives for consumers to spend on health care wisely.

7. Markets and Evolution

Here are four key points to consider:

- The traditional defense of markets is that they are an efficient way to allocate a given set of resources.
- The defense of markets that I find more compelling is that they facilitate innovation by forcing failed innovations and obsolete processes to disappear.
- The "learning paradigm" view of markets sees innovation by trial and error as the most valuable economic process. Government intervention tends to be inimical to such innovation.
- If government takes over health care, then special interests, particularly doctors and other medical suppliers, will steer regulations to maintain their incomes.

As noted in Chapter 4, American cultural expectations will have to change to rein in health care costs. If we place health care supply under the direction of a national government budget, then Americans' expectations for availability and unfettered access to health care will be thwarted. If we go in the other direction, encouraging market forces to control health care, then that means removing much of the insulation from health care costs to which most Americans have become accustomed.

I believe that it would be better to move in the direction of decentralized markets than in the direction of a national health care budget. I think it would be better to challenge Americans' cultural preference for insulation than to challenge our cultural preference for unfettered access. My reason is that over time market systems evolve, improve, and discard failed methods. Government-run systems tend to stagnate and adapt less readily.

Markets are conducive to evolutionary improvement. Government empowers those who want to resist change. For me, this is the most compelling reason to allow markets to play a significant role in paying for health care. As I see it, we do not know how to achieve an optimal allocation of resources in health care. However, we can improve an imperfect system through gradual, trial-and-error learning. That learning takes place more easily when political forces are held in check.

Three Views of Markets

One may draw a contrast between three views of markets:

- A noneconomic view is that competition is wasteful, profits are an unnecessary evil, and government will run industries more efficiently and fairly.
- The standard paradigm in economics looks at equilibrium outcomes of a market economy and compares those outcomes with outcomes of government intervention.
- Another economic paradigm looks at the process of growth and change.

The Noneconomic View

Historical experience provides little support for the noneconomic paradigm. State-run industries tend to be inefficient. They allocate capital unwisely. They generate shortages in some areas while they waste resources in others.

The noneconomic view of drug companies is that without profits and advertising they would have more money to spend on drug discovery. The economic view is that the money to spend on drug discovery comes from the expectation of earning a return. Without advertising and profits, there is no return on investment and no drug discovery.

The noneconomic view of health insurance companies is that competition produces unnecessary cost and overhead. When there are many companies, each firm spends resources on functions that duplicate those of other firms. The economic counter-argument is that duplication occurs in any industry with multiple suppliers, but the advantages of competition typically outweigh the disadvantages of duplication.

Equilibrium Economics

Standard economic analysis is based on the concepts of optimization and equilibrium. Optimization means that individuals seek to maximize their well-being. Equilibrium is a "resting place" toward which the economy moves as a result of optimization. In equilibrium, firms have maximized profits and consumers have maximized their well-being, subject to the constraints of available resources and to the competitive behavior of one another. The standard approach to economic analysis of public policy is to compare the likely equilibrium with and without the policy.

The equilibrium paradigm could be described as a board game. With each turn, consumers and firms make choices based on the constraints that they face. When all apparent opportunities for mutually profitable exchange among all parties are exhausted, we declare that we have reached equilibrium and the turn ends. Then, we pick from a pile of "disturbance" cards. A card might read "A country that was previously closed to trade now opens up," or "The government raises the tax on gasoline," or some other disturbance. Then a new turn begins, consumers and firms make new choices, and we reach a new equilibrium. For example, in health care, one disturbance card might read, "The government subsidizes health insurance to everyone." How does the resulting equilibrium compare with one in which the government provides no health insurance?

The standard analysis would say that with government-subsidized health insurance, the amount of health insurance will be higher than if there were no subsidy. That in turn will raise the demand for health care above what it would have been otherwise. The quantity of services consumed and the price of health care services will be higher than would be the case without the subsidy.

The standard paradigm can be used to illustrate potentially undesirable outcomes in health care markets. In particular, once insurance coverage expires for someone with a chronic illness, it may be prohibitively expensive for that person to obtain new health insurance. Overall, the standard economic paradigm raises the question of how well private health insurance can protect the poor and the sick.

The Learning Paradigm

The final economic paradigm looks at the process by which the economy evolves and the standard of living grows over time. This might be called the "learning economy" paradigm, because it describes the economy as a learning mechanism. This paradigm was articulated by economists Joseph Schumpeter and Friedrich Hayek. The fundamental economic question in the learning paradigm is

73

how we came to be so rich relative to our ancestors. I like to use the example, based on the calculations of Brad DeLong, of the fact that if one measures productivity in terms of bags of flour that can be obtained with three days' labor, one can produce more than 400 times as much today as we did 500 years ago.[1]

The value of average per capita output in the United States now is an order of magnitude higher than that of medieval Europe or that of the poorest countries today. This is not because we have allocated a fixed amount of resources to yield a better equilibrium. Rather, it reflects the combination of (1) better scientific and technical knowledge with (2) an institutional framework that encourages applying science and technology to improve economic performance. That institutional framework includes property rights and decentralized market-based decisions.

We did not achieve these spectacular increases in our standard of living by reallocating what was known in 1500. Instead, it was exploring the unknown, trial-and-error, and the millions of discoveries and adaptations involved in that exploration that led to the production techniques and consumer goods and services that are available today. As the economy learns and adopts the better methods, we go from an inferior set of production techniques to a superior one. How to achieve this transition is a different problem from that of allocating a known set of resources.

The basic issue of what causes prosperity to emerge is not a question of how trading opportunities play out among a given array of goods. Instead, it is a question of how innovation takes place or does not take place and how institutional factors affect that process. Markets are part of the institutional framework that is conducive to sustained improvements in economic performance. That is because market competition rewards productive innovations, while forcing misguided innovations and obsolete methods to be discarded.

The standard economic paradigm is focused on static efficiency. From that perspective, markets serve to allocate resources, but this allocation is optimal only under a narrow and implausible set of assumptions, including perfectly informed consumers and unlimited competition among suppliers. Most real-world markets possess features that make them unlikely to produce such an optimum, even after all opportunities for profitable trades are exhausted.

When market conditions are imperfect, the standard paradigm may be used to analyze the "market failure." For example, in health care, consumers have imperfect information concerning the quality of advice that their doctors are providing, which makes it difficult for them to compensate doctors for quality of service. By taking a sufficiently optimistic view of government's ability to correct such "market failures," one can become quite expansive about the scope for government involvement in the economy.

In contrast, the learning paradigm is focused on change. If government takes over a function from the private sector, it might immediately eliminate a problem with the private-sector outcome on the basis of the equilibrium paradigm. However, any improvement is likely to be short-lived. Innovators no longer have the ability to challenge obsolete processes through competing products and services.

The learning paradigm sees innovation by trial and error as the most valuable economic process, and government intervention tends to be inimical to such innovation. Even when the market is producing unsatisfactory outcomes, my view is that eventually innovators will come along with better ideas. In that way, the market's errors tend to be self-correcting. Government's errors tend to perpetuate and to deepen.

Bureaucracies tend to resist innovation. In fact, in a corporate setting, that is their function. The corporation will be bombarded with proposals from other companies trying to establish business relationships. The corporation's own middle managers have many ideas for new projects that require time and capital. How can a company sift through all of these possibilities? The answer is bureaucracy. A corporation that tried to implement everyone's ideas would be like a venture capital firm that funded every business plan with which it was presented. Instead, the bureaucracy, which so frustrates every middle manager and every salesman who struggles to win a corporate account, is absolutely necessary to limit the company to undertaking a manageable, promising set of innovations.

All large organizations learn to resist innovation, even though individuals within those organizations may be highly creative. Occasionally, radical innovations emerge from a Bell Labs or a Defense Advanced Research Projects Agency or another large organization. However, those are exceptions. Bureaucracy is designed to limit experimentation, and government organizations tend to be particularly bureaucratic and change-resistant.

75

However, simply being large and bureaucratic is not the chief problem with government. The main way that government impedes innovation is by siding with those who are threatened by innovation. The incumbents in an industry always look to government for protection. When their wishes are granted, economic progress is thwarted.

When one sees a sector in the economy that lags in economic performance, in relation either to other sectors or to similar sectors in different countries, chances are that incumbent protection is at the root of the problem. In the United States, the biggest cost increases are in industries where government combines protection of incumbents against competition with subsidized demand. In health care, for instance, government regulates the practice of medicine. This is done in the name of consumer protection, but often it serves the purpose of walling off licensed professionals from competition.[2]

Once government takes over an industry, any innovation must pass through the political process. However, politics is dominated by interest groups, whose focus is on maintaining their incomes. In the case of health care, organizations such as the American Medical Association, which represent the interests of providers, are better organized than consumers to influence the political process.

In the noneconomic view, government represents "us" and private firms represent "them." Thus, nationalizing an industry is a triumph of the general interest over special interest. In the learning economy paradigm, private interests are held in check by other private interests. All forms of private economic advantage are temporary, as there are incentives for other private firms to compete with or innovate around firms that obtain market power. In the learning economy paradigm, nationalizing an industry slows the learning process, because it weakens consumers, strengthens special interests, and tends to solidify the status quo.

Future Challenges

The paradigm of what Schumpeter called "creative destruction"[3] and economic growth is increasingly relevant in the turbulent environment of health care in the 21st century. My reading of history is that rapid change cannot be managed centrally. Instead, what Hayek called "competition as a discovery procedure"[4] is better suited to navigating a rapidly changing technology landscape. Easy entry and exit of firms will ensure that good ideas succeed and resources are released from failed or outmoded processes.

The rise of premium medicine in the past 30 years has put a strain on our existing health care finance system. Today's "crisis of abundance" reflects increased specialization of medical skills along with the application of new technology relative to what was available 30 years ago. Assuming that the pace of change remains at least as high going forward, any reform that is designed to fit the health care of 2005 may be totally inappropriate for the health care of 2020 or 2030. Within 20 years, we may see

- Nanomedicine—the use of tiny devices that target small areas within the body
- Treatments tailored to genetic profiles
- Neuromedicine—the increased use of drugs and electronic devices to treat diseases of the brain and enhance mental performance
- Gene selection and/or replacement for newborns
- Telemedicine—diagnosis and treatment from a remote location—largely replacing in-person care

New health care technologies challenge boundaries in health care. For example, the boundary between what is an inevitable malady and what is a treatable illness shifts as new therapies emerge. The boundary between therapy and enhancement is also a moving line. Depression is much more widely diagnosed and treated today than it was even 20 or 30 years ago. Being in the lowest percentile for height is now considered a justification for hormone therapy to raise a youngster's physical stature. In the not-too-distant future, people probably will expect to be cured of social shyness, poor memory, unsatisfactory athletic ability, and so on.

To the extent that we want to foster adaptability to rapid technological change, it makes sense to maintain a large role for the private sector, with government limited to supporting basic research. For applied research and development, forces of competition maintain the pressure on private-sector systems to adapt to new realities. Firms that persist in obsolete processes will eventually lose money and go out of business. In contrast, government-controlled systems are much less capable of discarding failed models.

8. Policy Ideas

The growth of premium medicine poses a number of challenges. In this chapter, I offer some policy suggestions to meet those challenges. Some of these recommendations have been discussed in earlier chapters. They are not detailed legislative proposals. They are intended instead to be ideas for consideration.

1. Try to shift gradually the burden of health care spending for the elderly away from government and back to individuals. Policies to do this include the following:
   - Gradually raise the age of eligibility for Medicare.
   - Encourage health savings accounts.
   - Reduce incentives for those with means to use Medicaid to pay for nursing home care.
   - Encourage more careful evaluation of the costs and benefits of medical procedures.
   - Establish a Medical Guidelines Commission to coordinate research and recommendations for medical protocols.
2. Encourage innovation and efficiency in the market for health insurance.
   - Treat employer-provided health insurance as taxable income, or at least put a cap on the amount of health insurance benefits that may be provided tax free.
   - Eliminate barriers to offering health insurance policies across state lines.
   - Eliminate barriers to offering cumulative catastrophic health insurance, event-based insurance, or other potential solutions to the problem of illnesses with long-term expense profiles.
3. Encourage innovation in the provision of medical care by deregulating the health care sector.
   - In order to achieve integration of health care data, the health supply system probably needs to evolve toward single-point

accountability. If accountability for the patient's overall treatment remains diffuse, then information systems are unlikely to improve.
- Licensing restrictions on health care supply might be eased.

The Elderly

Insulating the elderly from health care costs is very popular, but very expensive.

- As of 2005, the payroll taxes for Medicare are less than the benefits being paid for hospitalization under Medicare. Over the next 75 years, Medicare expenditures are projected to grow faster than dedicated revenues. The present value of Medicare's deficits over those 75 years is $29.9 trillion.[1] That is more than five times the size of the projected deficits for Social Security.[2]
- In 1970, the average enrollee could expect to spend 16 years on Medicare. Because longevity has increased while the eligibility age remained fixed, this has lengthened to 18 years today and is expected to lengthen to 20 years by 2030.[3]
- Medicare spending is less than three percent of GDP today, but it is projected to increase rapidly, to 9.25 percent of GDP by 2050.[4]

The federal government has also attempted to calculate the present value of all future unfunded liabilities (not stopping at 75 years). The total, including the major entitlement programs, is about $81 trillion. The largest component by far is Medicare, with a present value unfunded liability of more than $68 trillion.[5]

The elderly also have a significant impact on the budget for Medicaid. It is estimated that in fiscal year 2003, about one-third of Medicaid's budget went for long-term care. That is, total Medicaid spending was $275.5 billion. Long-term care spending was $95.9 billion. Nursing home spending alone was $44.6 billion. By comparison, regular inpatient hospital spending in Medicaid was $36.1 billion .[6]

To prevent spending on health care for the elderly from swallowing most of the federal budget and a dangerously high share of GDP, Medicare and that portion of Medicaid that pays for long-term care need to be scaled back. In an earlier chapter, I pointed out that providing real health insurance to the elderly does not require paying all of their medical expenses. I suggested a combination of personal saving and Remaining Lifetime Catastrophic Insurance.

I propose a gradual transition away from Medicare and Medicaid toward private savings and appropriate insurance. In Chapter 7, I suggested phasing out Medicare by gradually raising the age of eligibility. I sketched a proposal for Remaining Lifetime Catastrophic Insurance that could protect the elderly from extraordinarily high health care expenses. Medicaid's eligibility rules for long-term care reimbursement need to be restructured. As it stands today, two people who enjoy healthy working lives and make different choices concerning consumption and saving receive perverse rewards. The spendthrift obtains Medicaid coverage for a nursing home, and the saver must pay entirely out of pocket.

Instead of our current approach, health savings accounts ought to be encouraged. Perhaps they should be mandatory, so that every individual will have at least $100,000 in savings in 2005 purchasing power by the time he or she reaches age 65. As noted earlier, the goal of $100,000 can be reached by saving $1,600 per year between age 30 and age 65, and can be augmented by other assets.

Medical Guidelines Commission

Chapter 5 discussed why health providers might prefer insulation. The current health care finance system tends to insulate both consumers and doctors from having to consider the cost of treatment, in part because of the way that physicians are paid. In the United States, the primary method is reimbursement for procedures. There is virtue in this approach. The consumers who require the most time and effort from doctors are the very sick. Reimbursing doctors for procedures ensures that they have an incentive to treat the sick, rather than attempt to "skim the cream" by only seeing healthy patients.

The problem with compensating doctors for procedures is that it does not provide an incentive to make treatment cost-effective. Procedures that have little or no bearing on the outcome may be just as reimbursable as essential health care. On the other side of the coin, errors of omission, in which health care providers fail to provide procedures that would be consistent with best practices, also do not adversely affect providers' incomes. In fact, errors of omission can often increase providers' incomes.[7] In short, compensating health care suppliers on the basis of reimbursement for procedures does nothing to promote quality.

The idea of compensating health care providers on the basis of quality has received increased attention in recent years. A number of initiatives are under way in many countries to try to implement "evidence-based medicine." In the United States, Medicare and many private plans have initiatives under way dubbed "pay for performance."[8] Compensation based on quality would be easy to implement—if it were simple to measure quality. In practice, it is the measurement problem that is the most difficult. Probably the most useful indicator of quality would be a measure of a health care provider's adherence to best practices. Doctors who regularly follow best practices should be rewarded more highly than doctors who frequently fail to follow best practices.

As noted in Chapter 3, it takes statistical and economic analysis to determine what constitutes best practice. Perhaps under a health care system in which more expenditures were paid out of pocket, consumer demand for information would be sufficient to induce private companies to undertake the necessary data-gathering and analysis. However, this might be a situation in which a "public good" market failure could arise due to difficulties a private firm might have in keeping the information it gathers from being freely redistributed by others. In any case, under our existing health care finance system, with consumers largely insulated from medical expenses, there is not sufficient incentive for consumers to concern themselves with costs and benefits.

Accordingly, I would recommend that the government charter a Medical Guidelines Commission that would undertake the research and analysis needed to develop guidelines for best practices. The commission would incorporate the expertise of medical practitioners and also that of statisticians and economists.

The United Kingdom has a similar sort of commission called the National Institute for Health and Clinical Excellence. The institute is particularly powerful under the health care system in Britain, where the National Health Service makes spending decisions subject to government budget rules.

In the United States, the commission's guidelines would be influential but not dictatorial. The commission might offer guidelines as to when to order an MRI for lower back pain, or for how frequently a patient with a particular heart condition ought to be seen by a cardiologist. Today, these sorts of decisions are made on the basis of habit and convenience, rather than on the basis of evidence. To minimize the effect that guidelines might have on reducing the doctors' ability to choose the treatment they think is best, the commission would have to strike a balance that allows for flexibility. In circumstances where a number of treatment options are reasonable, the guidelines should reflect this.

Patients and doctors would be free to make choices that deviate from the guidelines. However, health insurance policies might be designed to use the guidelines to set expectations for the cost of treatment, so that if a more expensive treatment is chosen, only a portion (or none) of the additional cost would count toward meeting the deductible. Thus, just as consumers in some health care plans have to pay more if they go with an "out of plan" provider, they might have to pay more if they seek an "out of guideline" treatment. Medicare and other insurers experimenting with pay for performance would use the guidelines to influence compensation. They could provide a basis for penalizing errors of omission as well as errors of commission.

Finally, guidelines might serve to make medical malpractice suits less arbitrary. Physicians would have clearer signals about what is standard medical practice, and courts could use guidelines as one factor in establishing a standard of care.

The idea of a commission to oversee and evaluate research on the costs and benefits of medical protocols has been proposed before. For example, Victor Fuchs, in the policy journal *Health Affairs*, wrote in October 2004:

> Given the rapid rate of introduction of new medical technologies and the consequent rapid growth of health spending, there is urgent need for a large, private, nonprofit institution to assess the cost-effectiveness of various interventions. It must have a large, steady source of funding and be as free from political and professional pressures as possible. Its primary function would be to help develop and disseminate systematic knowledge about the cost-effectiveness of medical technologies, including drugs, diagnostic procedures, and surgical interventions. Its second important function would be to provide legitimacy for the cost-effective practice of medicine. Many directors of health plans and many physicians know that they could be practicing in a more cost-effective way, but they are inhibited from doing so by fear of malpractice suits and by pressure from patients and peers.[9]

Earlier, in the Winter 2003 issue of the *Brookings Review*, Fuchs and Alan M. Garber had written:

> We recommend creating a National Center for the Assessment of Medical Technologies, with an annual budget of $1 billion, financed by a small levy (less than one-tenth of 1 percent) on all health care spending. The National Center would sponsor and conduct research and serve as a repository for diverse data and health information. It would help develop and disseminate systematic knowledge about the effectiveness and value of medical technologies, providing the information that health care providers and patients need to make decisions about when to use both new and established technologies.[10]

My own recommendation would be for a gradual evolution toward a well-funded, permanent commission. In the meantime, a pilot program would provide a more cautious approach. The Medicare pay-for-performance initiative, referred to earlier, might serve as such a pilot.

It would be important to keep the commission independent of political pressures. Consumers and pharmaceutical companies are protesting a recent decision by the United Kingdom's National Institute for Health and Clinical Excellence.[11] If the process is politicized, then that undermines the goal of measuring costs and benefits objectively. For that reason, a private-sector approach would be preferable. As noted previously, a private market for research on the cost-effectiveness of medical practices is more likely to emerge under a regime in which consumers are less insulated from health care costs than they are today.

Remove Distortions in Private Health Insurance

To economists, catastrophic health insurance makes more sense than conventional health coverage. We believe that consumers will be more careful about how they spend on health care if more of their low-dollar payments are made out of pocket. Real health insurance would protect people against the costs of expensive illnesses, not against everyday medical bills. Of course, consumers may prefer comprehensive insurance that pays all bills, regardless of size and regardless of overall spending. People should not be denied the right to purchase such insurance.

My policy recommendation concerning health insurance is that government should not tilt the balance in favor of one type of coverage. Government distorts the insurance market, because regulations and tax policy encourage insulation over insurance. Employer-provided health insurance is not counted as taxable income. This produces a number of distortions. It makes health insurance relatively less expensive for people who work for large companies than for those without access to employment-based insurance. It also encourages people to take income in the form of health insurance, which in turn encourages them to take forms of health coverage that are more comprehensive and more costly than catastrophic coverage.

Some reformers are concerned solely with creating a "level playing field" between those who do and do not have access to employer-sponsored insurance. In that case, providing a tax deduction for individuals to obtain health insurance is an option. However, it could extend the distortion that favors excessive health coverage. The concern I have is that the tax subsidy creates an incentive to go beyond catastrophic health insurance. If employer contributions to health insurance were treated as income for tax purposes, then no one would have a tax incentive to obtain excessive health coverage. The choices that people make would not be distorted.

A less radical approach would be to cap the amount of tax-free income that individuals may receive in the form of health insurance. Health economist Robert B. Helms suggests:

> For example, if the cap were placed at $6,000 per year, an employer providing a policy costing $8,000 would have to report $2,000 as taxable income for the employee. . . . The primary rationale for a tax cap is that it would remove the present open-ended incentive for employees, unions, and employers to keep adding tax-free health benefits relative to taxable wages. Primarily, this would give both firms and insurance companies stronger incentives to design more cost-effective policies.[12]

Helms points out that a cap on tax-free health benefits could be phased in gradually. In addition, if the cap were indexed to overall inflation (but not to health care inflation), then it would tend to become more binding as the relative cost of health care rises. As the cap becomes more binding, that increases the incentive for workers to choose catastrophic health insurance or other cost-effective policies.

Health insurance is part of interstate commerce, but different laws and regulations make it difficult or impossible to offer the same policy to consumers in different states. If consumers were able to shop for health insurance in any state, that might solve the problem.

Finally, regulators should not impede health insurers from offering innovative forms of coverage. For example, critical-care insurance, which provides lump-sum payments to people diagnosed with particular illnesses, is a promising innovation. In contrast to insurance that reimburses doctors for procedures, critical-care insurance would appear to require lower claims-processing costs and to maintain the incentive to choose treatment in a cost-effective manner.

Single Point of Accountability

When it comes to my checking account, my bank provides a single point of accountability. All checks that I write go through my bank. The bank's records of my financial transactions are definitive.

With a few exceptions, such as Kaiser Permanente or the Veterans Administration, there is no single point of accountability in health care. Once a patient leaves a hospital, that hospital's responsibility for that patient's continued well-being is minimal. The primary care physician has little or no accountability for care that takes place outside his or her office. The patient might self-refer to a specialist without informing anyone else who is involved in his or her health care.

Medical records are scattered in different locations and in different file formats. This leads to redundant clerical work and can even contribute to errors in treatment. It also is a contributing factor in the absence of usable information for consumers to compare doctors.

Health care's weak information systems should not be viewed as an isolated problem. In my career in business, I never saw a significant discrepancy between the way a business process was organized and the way its information systems performed. That is, I never saw a poorly functioning information system attached to a well-planned business process, or vice-versa. It is my belief that the driving factor in information systems is business organization. Business processes get the information systems they deserve.

What this view means for health care is that the fragmented character of patient records ought to be viewed as a symptom of problems with the business process, rather than as the fundamental cause of such problems. I suspect that the systems are fragmented because health care supply is fragmented.

Health maintenance organizations (HMOs), because they encompass a broad range of services, are in a position to provide something closer to single point of accountability. They are more likely to have modern, effective information systems. If a single point of accountability offered substantial improvements in health care efficiency, then one would expect HMOs to offer superior value per dollar in health care. If that were the case, consumers might be switching to HMOs at a more dramatic rate than what we observe.

Overall, I am skeptical that government—or a private entrepreneur—can "fix" the information systems in health care if the business remains fragmented. My guess is that attempts to standardize and computerize patient records will prove more costly and less beneficial than their proponents forecast. First, the issue of fragmented accountability must be addressed. However, it is not clear how government policy can contribute to moving health care in the direction of a single point of accountability. If there is a way for government to use pilot programs or experiments to stimulate standardization of medical records, then that might be a reasonable approach. As with the Medical Guidelines Commission, I would prefer to see a small pilot program first, rather than a commitment to a large program without having had a chance to experience the pitfalls of a concept.

Licensing Restrictions

Another possible source of inefficiency comes from government licensing restrictions and related regulations. If there is a shortage of, say, physical therapists, it is difficult for the market to remedy the shortage because of the many hurdles to obtaining a license. Professional regulation in medical care appears to be carried out in the interests of suppliers who wish to restrict competition. Consumer-oriented regulation instead would rely more on disclosure and less on restricting people's choices. That is, those who wish to practice physical therapy without all of the education requirements would be permitted to do so, with disclosure of the gaps in their training. The courts would continue to protect patients from willful or negligent harms.

Conclusion

Government may not have a solution for the "crisis of abundance" in health care. Government is part of the problem in that it spends scarce tax resources on the affluent elderly, rather than staying focused on providing for the health care needs of the poor. Policies that encourage employer-provided health insurance at the expense of individual insurance, and policies that encourage comprehensive health coverage instead of true health insurance, also drive up costs and increase the proportion of income that is devoted to health care.

The policy ideas presented here are more for illustration than for implementation. They show the general direction that is warranted by an economic analysis of our health care system, but they are not meant to be legislative proposals.

The goal of this book is not to offer a package of solutions. It is to raise the level of understanding of the realities, issues, and tradeoffs pertaining to health care policy. My biggest concern today is that the ratio of signal to noise in most health care policy discussions is quite low. Until the quality of analysis improves, health care policy will get worse rather than better.

Notes

Introduction

1. Mark Siegel, "Stopping an Elusive Killer," *Washington Post*, June 28, 2005, sec. HE01, http://www.washingtonpost.com/wp-dyn/content/article/2005/06/27/AR2005062701108.html.

2. David M. Cutler and Ellen Meara, "Changes in the Age Distribution of Mortality over the 20th Century," NBER Working Paper no. W8556, September 2001, http://post.economics.harvard.edu/faculty/dcutler/papers/cutler_meara_boulders_2001_final.pdf.

3. Note, however, that University of Pennsylvania health economist Mark Pauly has proposed that Medicare's financial future could be ensured if the program were changed so that it covered new technologies for the poor, but required nonpoor beneficiaries to purchase coverage for new technologies themselves. See Pauly, "Means-Testing in Medicare," *Health Affairs Web Exclusive*, December 8, 2004, p. W4-546, http://content.healthaffairs.org/cgi/content/abstract/hlthaff.w4.546v1.

Chapter 1

1. Quixote, "Shoot Me Now: 'Health Care' in the New Millennium," *Acid Test*, April 11, 2005, http://acid-test.blogspot.com/2005/04/shoot-me-now-health-care-in-new.html.

2. Centers for Disease Control, National Center for Health Statistics, *Health, United States, 2004* (Hyattsville, Maryland: 2004), p. 310, http://www.cdc.gov/nchs/data/hus04trend.pdf.

3. Barbara Starfield et al., "The Effects of Specialist Supply on Populations' Health: Assessing the Evidence," *Health Affairs Web Exclusive*, March 15, 2005, http://content.healthaffairs.org/cgi/content/abstract/hlthaff.w5.97.

4. Annetine C. Gelijns et al., "Evidence, Politics, and Technological Change," *Health Affairs* 24, no. 1 (January/February 2005), http://content.healthaffairs.org/cgi/content/full/24/1/29.

5. Todd A. Gould, "How MRI Works," HowStuffWorks, http://electronics.howstuffworks.com/mri.htm.

6. Gail Prochaska, "Latest IMV Study Shows MRI Clinical Utilization Expanding," *IMV, Limited*, April 19, 2005, http://www.imvlimited.com/PDF/2005/MID/Press%20Release/MRI04%20Release%20April05.pdf; and Gail Prochaska, "Latest IMV CT Census Confirms That CT Is the Workhorse of Radiology," *IMV, Limited*, February 4, 2005, http://www.imvlimited.com/PDF/2005/MID/Press%20Release/CT04%20press %20release.pdf.

7. F. A. Mettler Jr. et al., "Use of Radiology in U.S. General Short-Term Hospitals: 1980–1990," *Radiology* 189 (1993): 377–380, http://radiology.rsnajnls.org/cgi/content/abstract/189/2/377.

8. Mark E. Miller, "MedPAC Recommendations on Imaging Services," *Statement before the Subcommittee on Health, Committee on Ways and Means, U.S. House of Representatives*, March 17, 2005, http://www.medpac.gov/publications/congressional_testimony/031705-TestimonyImaging-Hou.pdf.

9. U.S. Medicare Payment Advisory Committee, "Ambulatory Care," *A Data Book: Healthcare Spending and the Medicare Program*, June 2005, p. 143, http://www.medpac.gov/publications/congressional_reports/Jun05DataBookSec9.pdf.

10. David M. Studdert et al., "Defensive Medicine among High-Risk Specialist Physicians in a Volatile Malpractice Environment," *Journal of the American Medical Association* 293, no. 21 (June 1, 2005): 2609–2617, http://jama.ama-assn.org/cgi/content/abstract/293/21/2609.

11. Centers for Disease Control, National Center for Health Statistics, *Health Care in America: Trends in Utilization*, January 2004, p. 25, http://www.cdc.gov/nchs/data/misc/healthcare.pdf.

12. Jonathan Skinner and John E. Wennberg, "How Much Is Enough? Efficiency and Medicare Spending in the Last Six Months of Life," in David M. Cutler, ed., *The Changing Hospital Industry: Comparing Not-for-Profit and For-Profit Institutions* (Chicago: The University of Chicago Press, 2000), pp. 169–193.

13. John E. Wennberg, "Variation in Use of Medicare Services among Regions and Selected Academic Medical Centers: Is More Better?" *Duncan A. Clark Lecture: New York Academy of Medicine*, January 24, 2005, http://www.dartmouthatlas.org/lectures/NYAM_Lecture_FINAL.pdf.

14. Ibid.

15. Renee Twombly, "Recommendations Raise Workload Issues for Colon Cancer Screening," *Journal of the National Cancer Institute* 96, no. 5 (March 2004): 348–350.

16. Matt Ridley, *Genome* (New York: HarperCollins Publishers, 1999), p. 195.

17. Aubrey de Grey, interview by Phil Bowermaster, "Speaking of the Future with Aubrey de Grey," *The Speculist*, August 6, 2003. The alternative paradigm would leapfrog existing medical practice. However, at this point, it is little more than a gleam in the eyes of a few visionaries.

18. See, for example, Robert Fogel, *The Escape from Hunger and Premature Death, 1700–2100* (Cambridge: Cambridge University Press, 2004), p. 109.

Chapter 2

1. Tim Harford, *The Undercover Economist* (New York: Oxford University Press, 2006), p. 114.

2. See Mark Pauly and Bradley Herring, *Pooling Health Insurance Risks* (Washington, D.C.: The AEI Press, 1999).

3. Gaetan Lafortune, "Impact of Population Aging on Health and Long-Term Care Expenditure: Assessing the Effect of Morbidity, Disability and Other Cost Drivers," *OECD Workshop organized by the European Commission (Working Group on Aging) and the OECD*, February 21–22, 2005, http://europa.eu.int/comm/ economy_finance/events/2005/workshop0205/1en.pdf.

4. Gerard F. Anderson et al., "It's the Prices, Stupid: Why the United States Is So Different from Other Countries," *Health Affairs* 22, no. 3 (September/October 2003): http://content.healthaffairs.org/cgi/reprint/ 22/3/89.

5. Cynthia Smith et al., "Health Spending Growth Slows in 2003," *Health Affairs* 24, no. 1 (January–February 2005): 185–194.

6. David Cutler and others suggest that, if quality improvements are properly taken into account, then health care prices have actually been falling. See David Cutler, Mark McClellan, Joseph P. Newhouse, and Dahlia Remler, "Are Medical Prices Falling?" *Quarterly Journal of Economics* 113, no. 4 (November 1998): 991–1024.

7. See Jonathan Skinner and John E. Wennberg, "How Much Is Enough? Efficiency and Medicare Spending in the Last Six Months of Life," in David M. Cutler, ed., *The Changing Hospital Industry: Comparing Not-for-Profit and For-Profit Institutions* (Chicago: The University of Chicago Press, 2000), pp. 169–193.

8. Centers for Disease Control, National Center for Health Statistics, *Health, United States, 2004,* "Table 30—Years of Potential Life Lost before Age 75 for Selected Causes of Death, according to Sex, Race, and Hispanic Origin: United States, Selected Years 1980–2002" (Washington: Government Printing Office, December 2, 2004), p. 150, http://www.cdc.gov/nchs/data/hus/hus04trend.pdf.

9. Matt Ridley, *Genome* (New York: HarperCollins, 1999), p. 155.

10. Gabriele Doblhammer-Reiter and James W. Vaupel, "The Lifetime Legacy of Very Early Life," Max Planck Institute for Demographic Research, 2005, http://www.demogr.mpg.de/general/structure/division1/lab-sl/78.htm/.

11. Caleb E. Finch and Eileen M. Crimmins, "Inflammatory Exposure and Historical Changes in Human Life-Spans," *Science* 305, no. 5691 (September 17, 2004): 1736–1739, http://www.sciencemag.org/cgi/reprint/305/5691/1736.pdf?ijkey=040ce78b1d514ecf00e9f0df5d8e15ec5be361ef.

12. Robin Hanson, "Showing That You Care: The Evolution of Health Altruism," George Mason University Working Paper, November 2000, http://hanson.gmu.edu/showcare.pdf.

Chapter 3

1. The probability calculations can be quite intricate. When one undergoes an MRI, there may be several possible diagnoses. In theory, before undergoing an MRI, one could assign a probability to each possible finding that it could produce. After the MRI, there will be a choice of treatment plans based on the finding. The outcome of each treatment plan will be uncertain. Taking all of this into account makes the "expected value" of the original MRI very complex to compute.

2. David M. Cutler, *Your Money or Your Life: Strong Medicine for America's Healthcare System* (Oxford: Oxford University Press, 2004), pp. 16–17.

3. Gustav Quade, "Screening for Bladder and Other Urothelial Cancers," *German National Cancer Institute*, May 18, 2005, http://www.meb.uni-bonn.de/cancer.gov/CDR0000062875.html.

4. Carol A. Burke, "Colon Cancer," *The Cleveland Clinic*, June 12, 2003, http://www.clevelandclinic meded.com/diseasemanagement/gastro/colorectalneoplasia/colorectalneoplasia.htm.

5. O. D. Jorgensen et al., "The Funen Adenoma Follow-up Study. Incidence and Death from Colorectal Carcinoma in an Adenoma Surveillance Program," *Scandinavian Journal of Gastroenterology* 1993, no. 28: 869–874.

6. Ibid.

7. Medical Procedure News, "Virtual Colonoscopy Effective in Finding Most Polyps but May Miss Small Ones," ScanDirectory.com, April 21, 2005, http://www.scandirectory.com/news/news_details.asp?ID=67.

8. Statistics Canada, "Use of Mammograms among Women Aged 50 to 69, Canada and United States, 2002 to 2003," *Joint Canada/United States Survey of Health, 2002 to 2003*, http://www.statcan.ca/english/freepub/82M0022XIE/2003001/tables/table3.htm.

9. John E. Wennberg, "Variation in Use of Medicare Services among Regions and Selected Academic Medical Centers: Is More Better?" *Duncan A. Clark Lecture: New York Academy of Medicine*, January 24, 2005, p. 24, http://www.dartmouthatlas.org/lectures/NYAM_Lecture_FINAL.pdf.

Chapter 4

1. See Michael F. Cannon and Michael D. Tanner, *Healthy Competition: What's Holding Back Health Care and How to Free It* (Washington: Cato Institute, 2005).

2. David M. Cutler, *Your Money or Your Life: Strong Medicine for America's Healthcare System* (Oxford: Oxford University Press, 2004).

3. Public spending on health care is even more costly than government figures make it seem. Generally speaking, a dollar of taxes costs between $.20 and $.60 of GDP, because of what economists call the "deadweight loss" involved. (See U.S. Congressional Budget Office, *Budget Options*, February 2001, p. 381, http://www.cbo.gov/ftpdocs/27xx/doc2731/ENTIRE-REPORT.PDF.) The deadweight loss includes administrative costs of collection and compliance, as well as reductions in economic output as consumers respond to taxes by working and saving less. Thus, all else equal, funding health care out of public money rather than private money is very expensive. Spending public money on a health care procedure that costs $100 reduces the resources that could be spent elsewhere by more than $120—the $100 cost of the procedure plus $20 or more in deadweight loss.

Chapter 5

1. John C. Goodman, "Health Insurance," *The Concise Encyclopedia of Economics*, 1993, http://www.econlib.org/library/Enc/HealthInsurance.html.

2. Author's calculations from "Table 9: Total Expenditure on Health, Per Capita US$ PPP," and "Table 16: Out-of-Pocket Payments, Per Capita US$ PPP," *OECD Health Data 2004—Frequently Requested Data*, June 3, 2004, author's files.

3. See John H. Cochrane, "Time-Consistent Health Insurance," *Journal of Political Economy* 103, no. 3 (1995): 445–473; and Alex Tabarrok, "Genetic Testing: An Economic and Contractarian Analysis," *Journal of Health Economics* 13 (1994): 75–91. Versions of these articles can be found in Tabarrok, ed., *Entrepreneurial Economics* (Oxford: Oxford University Press, 2002).

4. For an example of the latter, see my commentary on a piece by Malcolm Gladwell in the *New Yorker* (August 29, 2005): Arnold Kling, "How Economists Really View Health Insurance," *Tech Central Station*, August 26, 2005, http://www.techcentralstation.com/082605E.html.

5. Emmett B. Keeler, "Effects of Cost Sharing on Use of Medical Services and Health," *RAND Health* (Summer 1992): 317–321, http://www.rand.org/publications/RP/RP1114/.

6. "For example, for low-income persons with high blood pressure, free care brought better control of blood pressure (Brook et al., 1983). Free care reduced the risk of early death among those at high risk. Coverage of services such as vision care also made a difference; free-care individuals with poor vision were more likely to have vision correction." Karen Davis, "Consumer-Directed Health Care: Will It

Improve Health System Performance?" *Health Services Research* 39: 4, Part II (August 2004), p. 1221, http://www.cmwf. org/usr_doc/hsr_39_4p2_1219_Davis.pdf.

7. Note that Pauly and colleagues find that markets perform reasonably well at reducing "renewal risk." See Mark Pauly, "How Private Health Insurance Pools Risk," *NBER Reporter OnLine: Summer 2005*, September 15, 2005, p. 7, http://nber.org/reporter/summer05/pauly.html.

8. See John H. Cochrane, "Time-Consistent Health Insurance," *Journal of Political Economy* 103, no. 3 (1995).

9. A modification of this approach, which I mention in Chapter 6, would be to have the insurance policy pay 50 percent of expenses between $15,000 and $30,000 and 100 percent of expenses thereafter. In the example above, such a modification would mean that insurance pays $5,500 in 2009.

10. The data can be obtained at Agency for Healthcare Research and Quality. 2002 Full Year Consolidated Data File (HC-070), "Medical Expenditure Panel Survey (MEPS) Household Component," *MEPSnet*, December 27, 2004, http://www.meps.ahrq.gov/mepsnet/HC/MEPSnetHC.asp.

The MEPS data differ from the National Health Accounts, which show mean expenditures of more than $4,000 per capita (and total spending of $1.6 trillion) in 2002, for a variety of reasons. One major difference is that the MEPS data do not include the institutional population—people in nursing homes. For more information on differences between MEPS and NHA, see Thomas M. Selden et al., "Reconciling Medical Expenditure Estimates from the MEPS and the NHA, 1996," *Health Care Financing Review* 23, no. 1 (Fall 2001): 161–178.

11. Joanne Lynn and David M. Adamson, "Living Well at the End of Life: Adapting Health Care to Serious Chronic Illness in Old Age," *RAND Health*, June 14, 2003, http://www.rand.org/pubs/white_papers/ WP137/WP137.pdf.

12. Alastair Gray, "Population Ageing and Health Care Expenditure," *Ageing Horizons* 2 (2005): 15–20, http://www.ageing.ox.ac.uk/ageinghorizons/thematic%20issues/healthcare/papers%20healthcare/pdf%20files/gray%20issue%202%202005.pdf.

13. David M. Cutler and Richard Zeckhauser, "Extending the Theory to Meet the Practice of Insurance," Harvard University and National Bureau of Economic Research, April 2004, http://post.economics.harvard. edu/faculty/dcutler/papers/cutler_zeckhauser_theory_and_practice_of_insurance.pdf.

14. See exhibit 5 in Geoffrey F. Joyce et al., "The Lifetime Burden of Chronic Diseases Among the Elderly," *Health Affairs Web Exclusive*, September 26, 2005, W5–R18, http://content.healthaffairs.org/cgi/content/full/hlthaff.w5.r18/DC1.

15. David Cutler, "The Potential For Cost Savings In Medicare's Future," *Health Affairs* Web Exclusive, September 26, 2005, p. W5-R78, http://content.healthaffairs.org/cgi/reprint/hlthaff.w5.r77v1.pdf.

16. David Cutler, "Why Don't Markets Insure Long-Term Risk?" Harvard University and National Bureau of Economic Research, May 1996, http://post.economics.harvard.edu/faculty/dcutler/papers/ltc_rev.pdf.

Chapter 6

1. The astute reader will also notice that the ratio of spending on the elderly to spending on the nonelderly represented here ($7,509/$2,137 = 3.5) is lower than the ratio presented in Chapter 2 (4.0). The reason for this is that the MEPS data discussed here cover only the noninstitutional population. That means the MEPS data miss a

considerable amount of spending for the elderly in nursing homes. Including those expenditures on the institutional population brings the U.S. ratio closer to 4.0.

2. Note: In calculating actual sources of funding, private insurance includes the "other private" category of MEPS. All categories other than "self and family," "private insurance," and "other private" are considered government.

3. Rachel Emma Silverman, "Critical Care, the Industry's Latest Push," *Wall Street Journal*, July 14, 2005, sec. D1, http://online.wsj.com/article/0,,SB112129587930685155,00. html?mod=health%5Fhome%5Fstories.

Chapter 7

1. J. Bradford DeLong, "The Real Shopping-Cart Revolution," *Wired* 11, no. 3 (March 2003), http://www.wired.com/wired/archive/11.03/view.html?pg=5.

2. See, for example, U.S. Federal Trade Commission/Department of Justice, *Improving Health Care: A Dose of Competition*, July 23, 2004, ch. 2, p. 29, http://www.ftc.gov/ reports/healthcare/040723 healthcarerpt.pdf.

3. Joseph A. Schumpeter, *Capitalism, Socialism, and Democracy*, 3rd ed. (New York: Harper Torchbooks, 1950), p. 81.

4. F. A. Hayek, "Competition as a Discovery Procedure," *Quarterly Journal of Austrian Economics* 5, no. 3 (Fall 2002), p. 9, http://www.mises.org/journals/qjae/pdf/ qjae5 3 3.pdf.

Chapter 8

1. *2005 Annual Report of the Board of Trustees of the Federal Hospital Insurance and Federal Supplementary Medical Insurance Trust Funds* (Washington: Government Printing Office, March 23, 2005), pp. 60, 101, 112, http://www.cms.hhs.gov/publications/ trusteesreport/tr2005.pdf.

2. *2005 Annual Report of the Board of Trustees of the Federal Old-Age and Survivors Insurance and Disability Insurance Trust Funds* (Washington: Government Printing Office, March 23, 2005), p. 57, http://socialsecurity.gov/OACT/TR/TR05/tr05.pdf.

3. U.S. Congressional Budget Office, "Medicare's Long-Term Financial Condition," statement of Douglas Holtz-Eakin before the Joint Economic Committee, Congress of the United States, April 10, 2003, pp. 8–9, http://cbo.gov/showdoc. cfm?index=4161&sequence=0.

4. *2005 Annual Report of the Board of Trustees of the Federal Hospital Insurance and Federal Supplementary Medical Insurance Trust Funds*, p. 29.

5. *2005 Annual Report of the Board of Trustees of the Federal Hospital Insurance and Federal Supplementary Medical Insurance Trust Funds*, pp. 60, 101, 112; and *2005 Annual Report of the Board of Trustees of the Federal Old-Age and Survivors Insurance and Disability Insurance Trust Funds*, p. 57.

6. John Holahan and Arunabh Ghosh, "Understanding the Recent Growth in Medicaid Spending, 2000–2003," *Health Affairs Web Exclusive*, January 26, 2005, pp. W5–52, http://content.healthaffairs.org/cgi/ content/full/hlthaff.w5.52/DC1.

7. U.S. Medicare Payment Advisory Committee, *Report to Congress: Variation and Innovation in Medicare* 108 (2003), p. 108, http://www.medpac.gov/publications/ congressional_reports/June03_ Entire_Report.pdf.

8. Centers for Medicare & Medicaid Services, "Medicare 'Pay for Performance (P4P)' Initiatives," Fact Sheet, January 31, 2005, http://www.cms.hhs.gov/media/ press/release.asp?Counter=1343.

9. Victor R. Fuchs, "Perspective: More Variation in Use of Care, More Flat-of-the-Curve Medicine," *Health Affairs Web Exclusive*, October 7, 2004, http://content.healthaffairs.org/cgi/content/full/hlthaff.var. 104/DC2.

10. Victor Fuchs and Alan M. Garber, "Medical Innovation: Promises & Pitfalls," *Brookings Review* 21, no. 1 (Winter 2003): 44–48, http://www.brookings.edu/press/review/winter2003/fuchs.htm.

11. Jeanne Whalen, "Britain Stirs Outcry by Weighing Benefits of Drugs Versus Price," *Wall Street Journal*, November 22, 2005, p. A1, http://online.wsj.com/article_print/SB113262391535503741.html.

12. Robert B. Helms, "Tax Reform and Health Insurance," *AEI Online, Health Policy Outlook*, January 1, 2005, http://www.aei.org/publications/pubID.21921,filter.all/pub_detail.asp.

Index

About the Author

Arnold Kling is an adjunct scholar of the Cato Institute. After he received his Ph.D. in economics from the Massachusetts Institute of Technology, he worked as an economist at the Federal Reserve Board. He is the author of Learning Economics and blogs at www.econlog.econlib.org.

Cato Institute

Founded in 1977, the Cato Institute is a public policy research foundation dedicated to broadening the parameters of policy debate to allow consideration of more options that are consistent with the traditional American principles of limited government, individual liberty, and peace. To that end, the Institute strives to achieve greater involvement of the intelligent, concerned lay public in questions of policy and the proper role of government.

The Institute is named for *Cato's Letters*, libertarian pamphlets that were widely read in the American Colonies in the early 18th century and played a major role in laying the philosophical foundation for the American Revolution.

Despite the achievement of the nation's Founders, today virtually no aspect of life is free from government encroachment. A pervasive intolerance for individual rights is shown by government's arbitrary intrusions into private economic transactions and its disregard for civil liberties.

To counter that trend, the Cato Institute undertakes an extensive publications program that addresses the complete spectrum of policy issues. Books, monographs, and shorter studies are commissioned to examine the federal budget, Social Security, regulation, military spending, international trade, and myriad other issues. Major policy conferences are held throughout the year, from which papers are published thrice yearly in the *Cato Journal*. The Institute also publishes the quarterly magazine *Regulation*.

In order to maintain its independence, the Cato Institute accepts no government funding. Contributions are received from foundations, corporations, and individuals, and other revenue is generated from the sale of publications. The Institute is a nonprofit, tax-exempt, educational foundation under Section 501(c)3 of the Internal Revenue Code.

CATO INSTITUTE
1000 Massachusetts Ave., N.W.
Washington, D.C. 20001
www.cato.org